THREE
PLAYS

PLAYS BY ARTHUR KOPIT

Oh Dad, Poor Dad, Mamma's Hung You in the Closet
and I'm Feelin' So Sad

Indians

Wings

The Days the Whores Came Out to Play Tennis
and Other One-Act Plays

Nine
(book for musical)

End of the World with Symposium to Follow

Road to Nirvana

Phantom
(book for musical)

THREE PLAYS

ARTHUR KOPIT

A DRAMABOOK

HILL AND WANG

A division of FARRAR, STRAUS and GIROUX

NEW YORK

Hill and Wang
A division of Farrar, Straus and Giroux
19 Union Square West, New York 10003

Library of Congress Cataloging-in-Publication Data
Kopit, Arthur L..
   [Plays. Selections]
   Three plays / Arthur Kopit. — 1st ed.
      p. cm.
   Contents: Oh Dad, poor Dad, Mamma's hung you in the closet and I'm
feelin' so sad — Indians — Wings.
   ISBN 0-8090-1595-1 (paper : alk. paper)
   I. Title.
PS3561.O646A6   1997
812'.54 — dc21   97-7532

To my great friend, Arthur Wang,
who published the plays I most deeply loved when I
first fell in love with drama — and later, best of all,
became the publisher of mine

CONTENTS

Preface by Arthur Kopit
ix

Oh Dad, Poor Dad, Mamma's Hung You in the Closet
and I'm Feelin' So Sad
1

Indians
81

Wings
175

PREFACE

To the reader unfamiliar with my work, the three plays in this volume—my first full-length plays to be produced—could easily appear, at first glance, to share only one thing in common: they were all written by me. I can only say that, if they appear stylistically dissimilar, it is not by design. For better or worse, each of my plays has always insisted on its own particular, idiosyncratic approach, and I rarely have an inkling of what that will be until I begin.

Not that I'm unaware of what I'm doing when I write; I am *highly* aware. But it is the play that leads me, not me the play.

That being said, I believe these works are in fact more closely akin than they might seem, and "seem" is the key. For it strikes me now, and, oddly enough, only now, that the concept of what *seems*, in opposition to what *is*, is at the heart of them all.

For example, Madame Rosepettle, in *Oh Dad . . .* , would seem to want nothing but her son's well-being, but the way she goes about it essentially destroys him.

Similarly, in *Indians*, Buffalo Bill seems to have genuine regard for the Indians, yet what he does on their behalf is either ineffectual or hastens their decline.

And in *Wings*, Emily Stilson seems, to the world she once knew, so reduced (as the consequence of a stroke) as to be effectively nonexistent. But in fact the opposite is true.

I see other common elements as well: an instinct for the nonliteral, for theatricality, irony, the droll, the surreal. These I always knew. What I did not see so sharply is how fundamentally the problem of identity runs through all these plays.

In *Wings*, Emily Stilson can no longer recognize her name. What she can recall of her past feels unreal. She wonders who she is. And yet, ironically, her sense of self is what gets her through.

In *Oh Dad* . . . Madame Rosepettle calls her son, whose given name is Jonathan, either Albert or Edward or Robinson, which turns out to be the full name of his dead father—hardly a healthy situation for the boy.

And Buffalo Bill, whose real name is of course William Cody, begins to doubt who *he* really is, while the Indians in his Wild West Show find themselves facing a similar problem—for their act is the reenacting of their glory, and sometimes, to their horror, the fakery seems almost real.

When I say I did not see these common elements at the time I wrote these plays, I do not mean I was unaware of these themes and motifs; I was totally aware. But I was aware of them only on a play-by-play basis. Instinctively, out of a strange kind of fear, I have always avoided analyzing my work as a whole, preferring instead to proceed piece by piece, as if the current piece was the first I ever wrote. I think my fear—or, more precisely, my fearful *suspicion*—was that if I saw too clearly what drew me to my material, I might begin to proceed by conscious choice rather than instinct and passion. Surprise is what I'm after—my *own* surprise. If I know too much when I start, it limits the surprise.

So my plays always begin at least somewhat in the dark. Something is hidden. Hidden from *me*. I sense it. It could be about a character. Or the situation. Most important, though, I sense that this hidden "thing" matters to me in some special way. If I am right, then I figure it is bound to matter to others as well—though to how many I cannot say, and never even try to guess. (That is the extent to which I think about the audience when I write.) My task then is a simple one: to find what is hidden in the shadows, and bring it out into the light.

So I suppose it could be said, I write about what I do not know.

The first play in this volume, *Oh Dad, Poor Dad . . .*, was written in the summer of 1959. I was twenty-two at the time and had just graduated from Harvard College with a B.A. in, of all things, electrical engineering. (*I can still scarcely believe it!*) Engineering was in fact just about the last thing I intended to do. Playwriting had become my passion.

That passion had been kindled my sophomore year when one of my teachers, an immensely gifted man named Gaynor Bradish, made a startling offer to a group of students, all theater buffs, and I was one of them. Gaynor said that if any of us wrote a one-act play during our upcoming spring break, he would stage it.

STAGE it!

I remember asking him to repeat what he'd just said. As I'd thought, he had said nothing about his needing to "like" what we turned in. For Gaynor, just writing it was enough.

Well, how could one say no to an offer like that? So, during spring break, I wrote a one-act play called *The Questioning of Nick*.

Though I had been writing short stories since my freshman year, and loved it so deeply I could imagine nothing more exciting or fulfilling than spending the rest of my life *as* a writer, for some reason the process of writing was for me a constant struggle against self-consciousness. No matter what I wrote, I was always aware of myself *writing*. And I knew it showed; I needed no teacher to tell me that.

In contrast, from the very first line of dialogue, the play just flowed. Not only was there no self-consciousness, it was as if I weren't even there. Or, rather, I *was* there—but only to jot down what my characters said. I remember thinking: *This is what it should be like!*

And then Gaynor staged the play. The actors, with only a few days' rehearsal, had to hold their scripts. There were at most maybe twenty people watching. And yet, and yet . . .

It didn't matter. The audience was gripped. The piece *worked!* And in ways my writing had never worked before.

The next fall, *The Questioning of Nick* won a college-wide playwriting contest and was given a full and wonderful production. The response was enthusiastic. And I was ecstatic.

At the top of my list of happiest and most extraordinary moments in my life I would put, without hesitation, the night I met the woman who would become my wife, the birth of our three children, and that night, in that college dining hall, miraculously transformed into a theater, when I saw, without a doubt, what I would do for the rest of my life.

I was a playwright!

Over the next two years, I wrote plays, and more plays, and still more plays. Mostly they were one-acts. (The hell with engineering!) By the time I graduated, six of them had been produced. And so that summer I was feeling a bit cocky. And decided to enter one more playwriting contest.

Like the first one I had entered, this one was also sponsored by one of Harvard's undergraduate houses. And, like that one, it, too, promised a full production to the winning script. But there was a big difference. This one had a prize attached—*two hundred and fifty dollars!*

I thought: *If I can win this, I will be a professional writer!*

So there you are. The truth. Full disclosure. I wrote *Oh Dad . . .* for money.

Well, that isn't fully true. What is wholly true is this: In my wildest fantasies, it never, for so much as a nano-second, occurred to me that this odd play of mine had any professional or financial or long-term possibilities other than, perhaps, if I were lucky, that two-hundred-and-fifty-dollar prize. If the thought *had* occurred to me, I think I would have frozen.

Certainly I would have written a very different play—and one not nearly so good. For as I look back on *Oh Dad . . .* now, what to me is strongest about the play is its exuberance, its energy. Not a moment's caution anywhere. It's absolutely unrestrained. Not at all what one would write if one sat down to write a "commercial" play. And there of course is the lesson.

You can't write a commercial play, a *good* commercial play— by which I suppose I really mean a good play—by setting out to write one. You have to cleanse your mind of all such thoughts. It's actually not hard to do; playwriting—as opposed to screenwriting—is astoundingly self-cleansing. Let dreams of commercial success enter your mind as you are writing and you're done for. The play is doomed.

Plays have to spring from some purer kind of place.

The idea for *Oh Dad* . . . came from a seemingly trivial anecdote my mother told me when I got home from college that summer. (No, the play is not about my mother.) The story she related—which she found both amusing and puzzling—dealt with a friend of hers, a widow, rather more beautiful than merry, and the widow's (I thought) much too deeply adored eight-year-old son. They lived in our town. I knew them more than slightly, but not a whole lot more.

I will not describe the actual incident my mother told me about because I liked this woman, and never wanted to cause her any embarrassment. However, that being said, I will say this: the incident convinced me that the widow's poor son was absolutely done for—and I have since found out that he grew up just fine.

So there you are.

I will also say, the event my mother told me about bears hardly any literal relation to what goes on in my play. So you're not missing all that much.

But I can tell you this: the incident took place in Haiti, and that's really what drew my attention. Because I could not figure out what this particular, rather frightened woman was doing in a hot spot like that. It was just not the sort of place it seemed to me she would go to, not with her son, take my word for it.

So I guess you could say I wrote the play to find out why she was there.

The idea for *Indians* came to me in March 1966. I was living in Vermont at the time, working on a novel—which I put aside when the concept for *Indians* occurred.

The concept took hold of me in one startling moment.

It was late in the afternoon. I had just come back from town with two (I was about to discover) highly significant items, the mix of which produced the idea for the play.

The first item was *The New York Times*. The second was a new recording of Charles Ives's Fourth Symphony, which I had never heard.

So I settled down to read, and to listen.

In the Ives piece, two orchestras play simultaneously, in opposition to each other. On the one hand, you have a serene, almost seraphic music based on folksongs beloved by Ives, such as "Shenandoah" and "Columbia, the Gem of the Ocean," and then the violent assault of a marching band drowning it all out. The effect is startling, jarring, and deeply powerful.

It was while I was listening to this music that I came upon an article, tucked well back in the paper, which described a small, "unfortunate incident" in Saigon. Someone on the street had shouted "Vietcong!" and some of our soldiers had instantly opened fire, killing several passersby. Then a few of our soldiers ran into a hospital and, for reasons no one could explain, shot some bedridden people. Then some of them leaned out a window and shot some more people down on the street. In all, about fifteen people were killed.

And not one was Vietcong.

But that was not what really angered me. What angered me, what in fact made me I would say practically go berserk, was General Westmoreland's statement in reaction to this incident. What he said was: "In war, these things happen. And our hearts go out to the innocent victims of this."

Without Ives's cacophonous, darkly patriotic music blasting at me as I read Westmoreland's grotesque verbal nonsense, this gross insult to reason, I would not have had anything close to the rage that suddenly, totally overwhelmed me, and led me to think of this play.

For some time, I had believed that our involvement in Vietnam was the expression of some deep national madness, a real disease — but that our being there was not the disease itself but a *symptom* of this disease.

And I had wanted to write about this because I just didn't understand it: what *were* we doing there?

But I didn't know how.

And then, instantly, I did.

The tawdry Westmoreland quote set against Ives's complex swirling celestial music is what brought it about.

What I saw was that this had all happened before. And I thought of the Old West, and about the Indians and the White Man, and that what was happening to us in Vietnam was part of a struggle we had been fighting throughout our history with people we thought of as being spiritually, morally, economically, socially, and intellectually our inferiors.

I saw at once that I would write about that earlier time. I even saw the form: it would be a hallucinatory panorama, a kind of nightmare mosaic, based on exhaustive research, but not slavishly locked into any one historical account.

What the play was about of course was mythology; I saw that right away as well.

I came upon Buffalo Bill about a month into my research and immediately knew: *he was the man for me.*

The idea for *Wings* came to me in 1976. I will not go into the particulars here, but will leave them till later in this volume, in a preface to the play, which I wrote in 1978 for its initial publication.

Arthur Kopit
Wilton, Connecticut
January 1997

OH DAD, POOR DAD,

MAMMA'S HUNG YOU IN THE CLOSET

AND I'M FEELIN' SO SAD

A Pseudoclassical Tragifarce

in a Bastard French Tradition

Standard Book Number (clothbound edition): 8090-7420-6
Standard Book Number (paperback edition): 8090-1202-2
Library of Congress Catalog Card Number: 60-13996

Printed in the United States of America
Published in Canada by HarperCollins*Canada*Ltd
First Dramabook Printing, August 1960

To my mother

though not the inspiration for Madame Rosepettle,
a source of inspiration nonetheless

Oh Dad, Poor Dad, Mamma's Hung You in the Closet and I'm Feelin'
So Sad was presented at the Phoenix Theatre, New York, by arrangement with Roger L. Stevens, on February 26, 1962

Characters

Madame Rosepettle   Jo Van Fleet
Jonathan   Austin Pendleton
Rosalie   Barbara Harris
Commodore Roseabove   Sandor Szabo
Head Bellboy   Tony Lo Bianco
Bellboys   Jaime Sanchez
        Anthony Ponzini
        Ernesto Gonzalez
        Louis Waldon
        David Faulkner
        Barry Primus

Directed by   Jerome Robbins
Scenery by   William and Jean Eckart
Costumes by   Patricia Zipprodt
Lighting by   Thomas Skelton
Music by   Robert Prince

SCENE 1

A lavish hotel room in Havana, Cuba. Downstage center French windows open onto a large balcony that juts out over the audience. Upstage center are the doors to the master bedroom. At stage left is the door to another bedroom, while at stage right is the door to the suite itself. On one of the walls is hung a glass case with a red fire axe inside it and a sign over it that reads, "In Case of Emergency, Break."

The door to the suite opens and BELLBOYS NUMBER ONE *and* TWO *enter carrying a coffin.*

WOMAN'S VOICE [*From off stage*]. Put it in the bedroom!

BELLBOYS NUMBER ONE AND TWO [*Together*]. The bedroom. [BELLBOY NUMBER ONE *starts toward the bedroom at stage left.* BELLBOY NUMBER TWO *starts toward the bedroom at upstage center. The handles come off the coffin. It falls to the floor. The* BELLBOYS *freeze with horror.*]

WOMAN'S VOICE [*Still off stage*]. Fools!

Enter MADAME ROSEPETTLE, *dressed in black, a veil hiding her face.* JONATHAN, *a boy seventeen years old but dressed like a child of ten, enters directly behind her. He follows her about the room like a small helpless puppy trailing his master.*

MADAME ROSEPETTLE. Morons! Imbeciles!

BELLBOY NUMBER ONE. Uh . . . *which* bedroom, madame?

BELLBOY NUMBER TWO. Yes. *Which* bedroom?

MADAME ROSEPETTLE. *Which bedroom!?* They have the nerve to ask, which bedroom? The *master* bedroom, of course. Which bedroom did you think? [*The* BELLBOYS *smile ashamedly, bow, pick up the coffin and carry it toward the master bedroom.*] Gently! [*They open the bedroom doors.* MADAME ROSEPETTLE *lowers her face as blindingly bright sunlight pours out from the room.*] People have no respect for coffins nowadays. They think nothing of the dead. [*Short pause.*] I wonder what the dead think of them? Agh! The world is growing dismal.

The BELLBOYS *reappear in the doorway, the coffin in their hands.*

BELLBOY NUMBER ONE. Uh . . . begging your pardon, madame, but . . . but . . .

MADAME ROSEPETTLE. Speak up! Speak up!

BELLBOY NUMBER ONE. Well, you see . . .

BELLBOY NUMBER TWO. You see . . . we were curious.

BELLBOY NUMBER ONE. Yes. Curious. That is . . .

BELLBOY NUMBER TWO. What we mean to say is . . .

BELLBOY NUMBER ONE. Just *where* in your bedroom would you like us to put it?

MADAME ROSEPETTLE. Next to the *bed,* of course!

BELLBOYS NUMBER ONE AND TWO. *Of course.*

[*Exit,* BELLBOYS NUMBER ONE *and* TWO.

MADAME ROSEPETTLE. *Fools.*

There is a rap on the door to the suite.

BELLBOY NUMBER THREE [*Off stage*]. The dictaphone, madame.

MADAME ROSEPETTLE. Ah, splendid.

BELLBOY NUMBER THREE *enters carrying a dictaphone on a silver tray and black drapes under his arm.* BELLBOYS NUMBER ONE *and* TWO *leave the bedroom and exit from the suite, bowing fearfully to Madame Rosepettle as they leave.*

BELLBOY NUMBER THREE. Where would you like it placed?

MADAME ROSEPETTLE. Great gods! Are you all the same? The center table, naturally! One never dictates one's memoirs from *anywhere* but the middle of a room. Any nincompoop knows that.

BELLBOY NUMBER THREE. It must have slipped my mind.

MADAME ROSEPETTLE. You flatter yourself. [*He puts the dictaphone and drapes down on the table.*]

BELLBOY NUMBER THREE. Will there be anything else?

MADAME ROSEPETTLE. *Will there be anything else,* he asks!? Will there be anything else? Of course there'll be something else. There's *always* something else. That's one of the troubles with Life.

BELLBOY NUMBER THREE. Sorry, madame.

MADAME ROSEPETTLE. So am I. [*Pause.*] Oh, this talk is getting us nowhere. Words are precious. On bellboys they're a waste. And so far you have thoroughly wasted my time.

BELLBOY NUMBER THREE. Madame, this must end. I can take no more. I will have you know I am not a *common* bellboy. I am

a lieutenant. Notice, if you will, the finely embroidered stripes on
my hand-tailored sleeve. I am a lieutenant, madame, and being
a lieutenant am in charge of other bellboys and thereby entitled to
a little more respect from you.

MADAME ROSEPETTLE. Well, *you* may consider yourself a
lieutenant, lieutenant, but *I* consider you a *bore!* If you're going
to insist upon pulling rank, however, I'll have you know that I am
a tourist. Notice, if you will, the money. And being a tourist I am
in charge of you. Remember that and I'll mail you another stripe
when I leave. As for "respect," we'll have none of that around
here. We've got too many important things to do. Right, Albert?
[*Jonathan tries to speak but cannot.*] Rrrright, Albert?

JONATHAN. Ra . . . ra . . . ra . . . ra-right.

MADAME ROSEPETTLE. You may begin by picking up the drapes
you so ingeniously dropped in a lump on my table, carrying them
to the master bedroom and tacking them over the windowpanes. I
don't wear black in the tropics for my health, my boy. I'm in
mourning. And since the problems confronting civilization are
ultimately moral ones, while I'm here in Havana no single speck
of sunlight shall enter and brighten the mournful gloom of my
heart. [*Short pause.*] At least, not while I'm in my bedroom.
Well, go on, lieutenant, go on. Forward to the field of battle,
head high. Tack the drapes across my windows, and when my
room is black, call me in.

BELLBOY NUMBER THREE. Yes, madame.
[*He picks up the drapes and walks into the master bedroom.*

MADAME ROSEPETTLE. In Buenos Aires the lieutenant clicked his
heels when leaving. That's the trouble with these revolutionaries.
No regard for the duties of rank. Remind me, Edward, to decrease
my usual tip. [*JONATHAN takes a pad of paper out of his pocket
and writes with a pencil he has tied on a cord about his neck. To*

the hallway.] Well, come in, come in. Don't just stand there with your mouths hanging open.

BELLBOYS NUMBER ONE *and* TWO *and* FOUR *enter pushing heavy trunks before them.*

BELLBOY NUMBER ONE. Where would you like the stamp collection, madame?

MADAME ROSEPETTLE. Ah, your fantastic stamp collection, Robinson. Where should it be put?

JONATHAN. Uh . . . uh . . . uh . . .

MADAME ROSEPETTLE. Oh, stop stammering and speak up! They're only bellboys.

JONATHAN. Uh . . . um . . . um . . . ma . . . ma . . . ma-ma-ma-ma-ma . . . ma—maybe . . . in . . . in . . . in . . .

MADAME ROSEPETTLE. Will you stop this infernal stammering? You know what I think about it! I said, where would you like your fantastic stamp collection put? God knows it's a simple enough question. If you can't muster the nerve to answer, at least point. [*He points to a bureau in the room.*] The bottom drawer of the bureau. And be careful not to get your fingers on them. They stick. [*The* BELLBOYS *go to the bureau, open the drawer, and dump hundreds of loose stamps that had been in the trunk into the drawer.* MADAME ROSEPETTLE *dips her hand into the drawer and plucks out three stamps. She offers one to each of the* BELLBOYS.] Here, for your trouble: 1903 Borneo, limited edition. Very rare. Almost priceless.

The BELLBOYS *look disappointedly at their tips.* BELLBOY NUMBER THREE *returns from the master bedroom.*

BELLBOY NUMBER THREE. I'm terribly sorry, madame, but I find that—

MADAME ROSEPETTLE. I wondered when you'd ask. [*She takes a huge hammer from her purse and hands it to him.*]

BELLBOY NUMBER THREE. Thank you, madame. Thank you. [*He turns nervously and starts to leave.*]

MADAME ROSEPETTLE. Bellboy? [*He stops.*] The nails.

BELLBOY NUMBER THREE [*Flustered by his forgetfulness*]. Yes, of course. How foolish of me. [*She reaches into her purse again and takes out a fistful of nails which she promptly dumps into his hands.*]

MADAME ROSEPETTLE. Keep the extras.

[*He exits into the master bedroom.* [*To Jonathan.*] In Buenos Aires the lieutenant came equipped with a pneumatic drill. Remind me, Albert dearest, to cut this man's tip entirely. [JONATHAN *scribbles on his pad. To the other* BELLBOYS.] Well?

BELLBOY NUMBER TWO. The . . . uh . . . coin collection, madame. Where would you like it put?

MADAME ROSEPETTLE. Your fabulous coin collection, Edward. Where should they put it?

JONATHAN. Uh . . . uh . . . I . . . I . . . I tha . . . tha . . . tha-think—

MADAME ROSEPETTLE. What is wrong with your tongue? Can't you talk like a normal human being without showering this room with your inarticulate spit!?

JONATHAN [*Completely flustered*]. I-I-I-I-I . . . I . . . da . . . da . . . don't . . .

MADAME ROSEPETTLE. Oh, all right, stick out your paw and point. [*He thrusts out his trembling hand and points again to the bureau.*]

JONATHAN. If . . . if . . . if . . . if they . . . if they would . . . be so . . . kind.

MADAME ROSEPETTLE. Of course they would! They're bellboys. Remember that. It's your first lesson in Life for the day. [*To the* BELLBOYS.] Next to the bottom drawer, bellboys. And make sure none of them gets in with his fantastic collection of stamps. [*From the master bedroom can be heard the sound of* BELLBOY NUMBER THREE *smashing nails into the wall. While the other* BELLBOYS *are busy dumping hundreds of loose coins into the bureau,* MADAME ROSEPETTLE *walks to the bedroom door and opens it, shielding her eyes from the blinding light.*] Don't bang, my boy. Don't bang. That's not the way. Just tap. It takes longer, I will admit, but the effect is far more satisfactory on one's auditory nerves—and my ears, you see, are extremely sensitive. [*To Jonathan.*] The lieutenant in Buenos Aires had a muffler on his drill. Remind me, Robinson darling, to have this man fired first thing in the morning. He'll never do. [JONATHAN *scratches a large "X" on his pad. The* BELLBOYS, *having finished dumping the coins, stand awaiting a tip.* MADAME ROSEPETTLE *goes to the drawer and takes out three coins. To* BELLBOY NUMBER ONE.] Here, for your trouble: a little something. It's a Turkish piaster . . . 1876. Good year for piasters. [*To* BELLBOY NUMBER TWO.] And for you an . . . an 1889 Danzig gulden. Worth a fortune, my boy. A *small* fortune, I will admit, but nevertheless, a fortune. [*To* BELLBOY NUMBER FOUR.] And for you we have a . . . a . . . a 1959 DIME!! *Edward* . . . what is a dime doing in here? Fegh! [*She flings the dime to the ground as if it had been handled by lepers. The* BELLBOYS *leap to get it.*]

JONATHAN [*Sadly*]. Some . . . some . . . someday it will be . . . as rare as the others.

MADAME ROSEPETTLE. Someday! *Someday!* That's the trouble
with you, Edward. Always an optimist. I trust you have no more
such currency contaminating your fabulous collection. H'm,
Albert? Do I assume correctly? H'm? Do I? H'm? Do I?
H'm? Do I?

JONATHAN. Ya . . . yes.

MADAME ROSEPETTLE. Splendid. Then I'll give you your surprise for the day.

JONATHAN. Na . . . now?

MADAME ROSEPETTLE. Yes, now.

JONATHAN. In . . . in . . . front of . . . *them?*

MADAME ROSEPETTLE. Turn your backs, bellboys. [*She digs
into her handbag and picks out a coin in a velvet box.*] Here,
Edward, my sweet. The rarest of all coins for your rarest of all
collections. A 1372 Javanese Yen-Sen.

JONATHAN [*Excitedly*]. How . . . how . . . how ma-many were
. . . ma-minted?

MADAME ROSEPETTLE. None.

JONATHAN. Na-none?

MADAME ROSEPETTLE. I made it myself. [*She squeezes his
hand.*] So glad you like it. [*She turns to the* BELLBOYS.] You may
turn around now. [*They turn around as a unit.*] Well, who
has the—? [*She stares in horror at the door to the master
bedroom. The tapping can clearly be heard. She goes to the
door, shielding her eyes from the now less powerful glare.*] You
are tapping and not banging, which is good, but when you tap

please tap with some sort of rhythm, which is, you see, much better. [*She smiles acidly and closes the door.*] The lieutenant in Buenos Aires, Robinson. The lieutenant in Buenos Aires. Do you remember him? Do you remember the rhythm he had? Oh, the way he shook when he drilled. I fairly danced that day. [*Reminiscent pause.*] Make note, Robinson. This man must be barred from all hotels, everywhere. Everywhere! [JONATHAN *retraces his "X" with a hard, firm stroke as if he were carving a figure on stone.*] Now where was I? Oh, yes. Forgive me, but my mind, of late, has been wandering. The books, bellboys. The books! [*The* BELLBOYS *push a large trunk forward.*]

JONATHAN. Ca . . . ca . . . could they . . . open it . . . I . . . I-I wonder?

MADAME ROSEPETTLE. You want to see them, eh Albert? You really want to see them again? That badly? You really want to see them again, that badly?

JONATHAN [*Trying very hard not to stutter*]. Yyyyesssssss.

MADAME ROSEPETTLE [*Very dramatically*]. Then let the trunk be opened! [*They open the trunk. Hundreds of books fall onto the floor in a cloud of dust.* JONATHAN *falls on top of them like a starved man upon food.*]

JONATHAN [*Emotionally*]. Tra-Tra . . . Trollope . . . Ha-Haggard . . . Dau-Dau-Daudet . . . Gautier . . . Tur-Tur-Tur-genev . . . ma-ma-my old fra-fra . . . friends. [*He collapses over them like a lover over his loved one.*]

MADAME ROSEPETTLE. Enough, Albert. Come. Off your knees Rise from your books and sing of love.

JONATHAN. But I . . . I ca-can't . . . sing.

MADAME ROSEPETTLE. Well, stand up anyway. [*He rises sadly.*] Now, where are my plants?

BELLBOY NUMBER TWO. Plants?

MADAME ROSEPETTLE. Yes. My plants. Where are they? [BELL-BOY NUMBER FOUR *whispers something in* BELLBOY NUMBER Two's *ear.*]

BELLBOY NUMBER TWO [*Laughing nervously*]. Oh. I . . . I . . . [*He laughs again, more nervously.*] I didn't realize . . . they were . . . plants.

MADAME ROSEPETTLE. What did you *think* they were?

BELLBOY NUMBER FOUR. We have them, madame. Outside.

BELLBOY NUMBER TWO. Yes. Outside.

BELLBOY NUMBER FOUR. Should we . . . bring them in?

MADAME ROSEPETTLE. Of course you should bring them in! Do you think they *enjoy* waiting out there in the hall? Fools.

BELLBOYS NUMBER TWO AND FOUR [*Together, weakly*]. Yes . . . madame.
They exit and return immediately carrying two large black-draped "things" before them at arm's length.

MADAME ROSEPETTLE. Ah, splendid. Splendid. Set them on the porch, if you will. [*They go out to the porch and set them down.*] Uh . . . not so close together. They fight. [*The* BELLBOYS *move the* PLANTS *apart.*]

BELLBOY NUMBER FOUR [*Weakly*]. Should we . . . uncover them?

MADAME ROSEPETTLE. No. That will be fine. Let the poor things rest awhile.

BELLBOYS NUMBER TWO AND FOUR [*Together, weakly*]. Yes . . . madame.

MADAME ROSEPETTLE. Now . . . who has my fish? [*All* BELL-BOYS *look toward the door.*]

A VOICE [*From outside the door*]. I have it, madame.
Enter BELLBOY NUMBER FIVE *carrying, at arm's length, an object covered by a black cloth. He wears large, thick, well-padded gloves—the sort a snake trainer might wear when handling a newly caught cobra.*

MADAME ROSEPETTLE [*With love in her voice*]. Ah, bring it here. Put it here, by the dictaphone. Near my memoirs. Bring it here, bellboy. Set it gently, then lift the shawl.

JONATHAN [*Staring sadly at his books*]. Sho-Sho-Sholo-Sholokhov . . . Alain-Fournier . . . Alighieri . . . ma-my ffffriends. [*The* BELLBOY *sets the object down.*]

MADAME ROSEPETTLE. The black shawl of mourning, bellboy. Remove it, if you will. Lift it off and drape it near its side. But gently. Gently. Gently as she goes. [*The* BELLBOY *lifts off the shawl. Revealed is a fish bowl with a* FISH *and a cat's skeleton inside.*] Ah, I see you fed it today. [*She reaches into her handbag and extracts a pair of long tongs. She plucks the skeleton from the fish bowl.*] Siamese, I presume.

BELLBOY NUMBER FOUR. No, madame. Alley.

MADAME ROSEPETTLE. WHAT!? A *common alley cat?* Just who do you think I am? What kind of fish do you think I have? *Alley cat! Alley cat!* The idea! In Buenos Aires, I'll have you know, Rosalinda was fed nothing but Siamese *kittens,* which are even more tender than Siamese cats. *That's* what I call consideration! Edward, make note: we will dismiss this creature from the bellboy squad *first thing in the morning!* [JONATHAN *scribbles on his pad.*]

BELLBOY NUMBER FOUR. Madame, please, there were no Siamese cats.

MADAME ROSEPETTLE. There are *always* Siamese cats!

BELLBOY NUMBER FOUR. Not in Havana.

MADAME ROSEPETTLE. Then you should have flown to Buenos Aires. I would have paid the way. Give me back your 1903 Borneo, limited. (I'll bet you've made it sticky.) [*He hands back the stamp.*] You can keep your Danzig gulden. It's not worth a thing except in Danzig, and hardly a soul uses anything but traveler's checks there anyhow! Shows you should never trust me.

BELLBOY NUMBER FOUR. Madame, *please.* I have a wife.

MADAME ROSEPETTLE. And *I* have a fish. I dare say there are half a million men in Cuba with wives. But show me another woman in Cuba with a silver piranha fish and then you'll be showing me something. Your marital status does not impress me, sir. You are common, do you hear? Common! While my piranha fish is *rare*. Now green piranhas can eat alley cats if they like; and red piranhas, I've been told, will often eat alley cats, tomcats, and even dogs; but my silver piranha has been weaned on Siamese, and Siamese it will be, sir. Siamese it will be. Now get out. All of you. There is much to do. Right, Albert?

JONATHAN. Ra . . . ra . . . ra . . . ra . . .

MADAME ROSEPETTLE. *Right,* Albert!?

JONATHAN. Ra-right.

ROSALINDA THE FISH [*Sadly*]. Glump.

MADAME ROSEPETTLE. Oh, dear thing. You can just tell she's not feeling up to snuff. *Someone will pay for this!*
Enter LIEUTENANT *of the bellboys from the bedroom.*

BELLBOY NUMBER THREE. Well, I'm finished.

MADAME ROSEPETTLE. You certainly are, *monsieur lieutenant*. You certainly are.

BELLBOY NUMBER THREE. I beg your pardon?

MADAME ROSEPETTLE. Make note, Edward. First thing in the morning we speak to the chef. Subject: Siamese cats—kittens if possible, though I seriously doubt it here. And make a further note, Albert, my darling. Let's see if we can't get our cats on the American Plan, while we're at it. [JONATHAN *scribbles on his pad of paper.*]

BELLBOY NUMBER THREE. Madame, is there something I can—?

MADAME ROSEPETTLE. QUIET! And put that hammer down. [*He puts it down. She puts it back in her purse.*] You have all behaved rudely. If the sunset over Guanabacoa Bay were not so full of magenta and wisteria blue I'd leave this place tonight. But the sunset *is* full of magneta and wisteria blue, to say nothing of cadmium orange and cerise, and so I think I'll stay. Therefore beware, bellboys. Madame Rosepettle will have much to do. Right, Robinson? [JONATHAN *opens his mouth to speak but no words come out.*] I said, *right Robinson?* [*Again he tries to speak, and again no words come out.*] RIGHT, ROBINSON!? [*He nods.*] There's your answer. Now get out and leave us alone. [*They start to exit.*] No. Wait. [*They stop.*] A question before you go. The yacht in the harbor. The pink one with the lilacs draped about the railing. One hundred and eighty-seven feet long, I'd judge. Who owns it?

BELLBOY NUMBER ONE. Commodore Roseabove, madame. It's a pretty sloop.

MADAME ROSEPETTLE [*Distantly*]. *Roseabove*. I like that name.

BELLBOY NUMBER ONE. He's a strange man, madame. A man who knows no master but the sea.

MADAME ROSEPETTLE [*With a slight smile*]. *Roseabove* . . .

BELLBOY NUMBER ONE. A wealthy man but a gentleman, too. Why I've seen him with my own eyes toss *real silver dollars* to the native boats as he sailed into port. And when some poor diver came to the surface without a coin glimmering in his hand, Commodore Roseabove, without the slightest hesitation, dropped a dollar bill instead. Oh he's a well-loved man, madame. A true, true gentleman with a big, big heart. A man who knows no master but the sea. And even the sea, they say, is no match for the commodore and his yacht, which, as you know, is the largest yacht in Cuba.

MADAME ROSEPETTLE. And also the largest yacht in Haiti, Puerto Rico, Bermuda, the Dominican Republic, and West Palm Beach. I haven't checked the Virgin Islands yet. I thought I'd leave them till last. But I doubt if I'll find a larger one there. [*She laughs to herself.*] I take great pleasure, you see, in measuring yachts. My hobby, you might say.

BELLBOY NUMBER ONE. Your hubby, did you say?

MADAME ROSEPETTLE [*Viciously*]. *Get out!* Get out before I lose my temper! *Imbeciles!* FOOLS!
[*They exit, running.*]
Edward, make note. First thing in the morning, we restaff this hotel. [JONATHAN *scribbles on his pad of paper.* MADAME ROSEPETTLE *walks over to the French windows and stares wistfully out.*

There is a short silence before she speaks. Dreamily, with a slight smile.] Roseabove. I like that name.

ROSALINDA THE FISH [*Gleefully*]. Gleep.

MADAME ROSEPETTLE [*Fondly*]. Ah, listen. My lovely little fish. She, too, is feeling better already.

Curtain.

SCENE 2

The place is the same. The time, two weeks later. JONATHAN *is in the room with* ROSALIE, *a girl some two years older than he and dressed in sweet girlish pink.*

ROSALIE. But if you've been here two weeks, why haven't I seen you?

JONATHAN. I've . . . I've been in my room.

ROSALIE. All the time?

JONATHAN. Yes. . . . All the time.

ROSALIE. Well, you must get out sometimes. I mean, sometimes you simply must get out. You just couldn't stay inside all the time . . . could you?

JONATHAN. Yyyyyes.

ROSALIE. You never get out at all? I mean, never at all?

JONATHAN. Some-sometimes I do go out on the porch. M-Ma-Mother has some . . . Venus'-flytraps which she bra-brought back from the rain forests of Va-Va-Va-Venezuela. They're va-very rrrrrare and need a . . . a lot of sunshine. Well sir, she ka-keeps them on the porch and I . . . I feed them. Twice a day, too.

ROSALIE. Oh.

JONATHAN. Ma-Ma-Mother says everyone must have a vocation in life. [*With a slight nervous laugh.*] I ga-guess that's . . . my job.

ROSALIE. I don't think I've ever met anyone before who's fed . . . uh . . . Venus'-flytraps.

JONATHAN. Ma-Ma-Mother says I'm va-very good at it. That's what she . . . says. I'm va-very good at it. I . . . don't know . . . if . . . I am, but . . . that's . . . what she says so I . . . guess I am.

ROSALIE. Well, uh, what . . . what do you . . . feed them? You see, I've never met anyone before who's fed Venus'-flytraps so . . . that's why I don't know what . . . you're supposed to feed them.

JONATHAN [*Happy that she asked*]. Oh, I fa-feed them . . . l-l-lots of things. Ga-ga-green peas, chicken feathers, rubber bands. They're . . . not very fussy. They're . . . nice, that way. Ma-Ma-Mother says it it it ga-gives me a feeling of a-co-co-complishment. Iffffff you would . . . like to to see them I . . . could show them to you. It's . . . almost fa-feeding time. It is, and . . . and I could show them to you.

ROSALIE. No. That's all right. [JONATHAN *looks away, hurt.*] Well, how about later?

JONATHAN. Do-do-do you ra-really wwwwwwant to see them?

ROSALIE. Yes. Yes I really think I would like to see them . . . later. If you'll show them to me then, I'd really like that. [JONATHAN *looks at her and smiles. There is an awkward silence while he stares at her thankfully.*] I still don't understand why you never go out. How can you just sit in——?

JONATHAN. Sometimes, when I'm on the porch . . . I do other things.

ROSALIE. *What?*

JONATHAN. Sa-sa-sometimes, when I'm . . . on the porch, you know, when I'm on the porch? Sssssssome-times I . . . do *other things*, too.

ROSALIE. What sort of things? [JONATHAN *giggles.*] What sort of things do you do?

JONATHAN. Other things.

ROSALIE [*Coyly*]. What do you mean, "Other things"?

JONATHAN. Other things besides feeding my mother's plants. Other things besides that. That's what I mean. Other things besides that.

ROSALIE. What kind of things . . . *in particular?*

JONATHAN. Oh, watching.

ROSALIE. Watching?

JONATHAN. Yes. Like . . . watching.

ROSALIE. Watching what? [*He giggles.*] *Watching what!?*

JONATHAN. You. [*Short pause. She inches closer to him on the couch.*]

ROSALIE. What do you mean . . . watching me?

JONATHAN. I . . . watch you from the porch. That's what I
mean. I watch you from the porch. I watch you a lot, too. Every
day. It's . . . it's the truth. I . . . I swear it . . . is. I watch you
ev-ry day. Do you believe me?

ROSALIE. Of course I believe you, Albert. Why—

JONATHAN. Jonathan!

ROSALIE. What?

JONATHAN. Jonathan. Ca-ca-call me Ja-Jonathan. That's my
na-na-na——

ROSALIE. But your mother said your name was—

JONATHAN. Nooooo! Call . . . me Jonathan. Pa-pa-please?

ROSALIE. All right . . . Jonathan.

JONATHAN [*Excitedly*]. You *do* believe me! You rrrrreally do
believe me. I-I-I can tell!

ROSALIE. Of course I believe you. Why shouldn't—?

JONATHAN. You want me to tell you how I watch you? You
want me to tell you? I'll bet you'll na-never guess.

ROSALIE. How?

JONATHAN. *Guess.*

ROSALIE [*Ponders*]. Through a telescope?

JONATHAN. How did you guess?

ROSALIE. I . . . I don't know. I was just joking. I didn't really think that was—

JONATHAN. I'll bet everyone watches you through a telescope. I'll bet everyone you go out with watches you through a telescope. That's what I'll bet.

ROSALIE. No. Not at all.

JONATHAN. Well, that's how I watch you. Through a telescope.

ROSALIE. I never would have guessed that—

JONATHAN. I thought you were . . . ga-going to say I . . . I watch you with . . . with love in my eyes or some . . . thing like that. I didn't think you were going to guess that I . . . watch you through a telescope. I didn't think you were going to guess that I wa-watch you through a telescope on the fa-first guess, anyway. Not on the *first guess*.

ROSALIE. Well, it was just a guess.

JONATHAN [*Hopefully*]. Do you watch *me* through a telescope?

ROSALIE. I never knew where your room was.

JONATHAN. Now you know. Now will you watch me?

ROSALIE. Well I . . . don't have a telescope.

JONATHAN [*Getting more elated and excited*]. You can make one. That's how I got mine. I made it. Out of lenses and tubing. That's all you need. Lenses and tubing. Do you have any lenses?

ROSALIE. No.

JONATHAN. Do you have any tubing?

ROSALIE. No.

JONATHAN. Oh. [*Pause.*] Well, would you like me to tell you how I made mine in case you find some lenses and tubing? Would you like that?

ROSALIE [*Disinterestedly*]. Sure, Jonathan. I think that would be nice.

JONATHAN. Well, I made it out of lenses and tubing. The lenses I had because Ma-Ma-Mother gave me a set of lenses so I could see my stamps better. I have a fabulous collection of stamps, as well as a fantastic collection of coins and a simply unbelievable collection of books. Well sir, Ma-Ma-Mother gave me these lenses so I could see my stamps better. She suspected that some were fake so she gave me the lenses so I might be . . . able to see. You see? Well sir, I happen to have nearly a billion sta-stamps. So far I've looked closely at 1,352,769. I've discovered three actual fakes! Number 1,352,767 was a fake. Number 1,352,768 was a fake, and number 1,352,769 was a fake. They were stuck together. Ma-Mother made me feed them im-mediately to her flytraps. Well . . . [*He whispers.*] one day, when Mother wasn't looking . . . that is, when she was out, I heard an airplane flying. An airplane . . . somewhere . . . far away. It wasn't very loud, but still I heard it. An airplane. Flying . . . somewhere, far away. And I ran outside to the porch so that I might see what it looked like. The airplane. With hundreds of people inside it. Hundreds and hundreds and hundreds of people. And I thought to myself, if I could just see . . . if I could just see what they looked like, the people, sitting at their windows looking out . . . and flying. If I could see . . . *just* once . . . if I could see *just once* what they looked like . . . then I might . . . know what I . . . what I . . . [*Slight pause.*] So I . . . built a telescope in case the plane ever . . .came back again. The tubing came from an old blowgun [*He reaches behind the bureau and produces a huge blowgun, easily a foot larger than he.*] Mother brought back from her last hunting trip to Zanzibar. The lenses were the lenses she had given me for my stamps. So I built it. My telescope. A telescope so I might be able to see. And . . . [*He walks out to the porch.*] and . . . and I *could* see! I could! I COULD! I really could. For miles and miles I could see. For miles and miles and *miles!* [*He begins to lift it up to look through but stops, for some reason, before he's brought it up to his eye.*] Only . . . [*He hands it to* ROSALIE. *She takes it eagerly and scans the horizon and the sky. She hands it back to him.*]

ROSALIE [*With annoyance*]. There's nothing out there to see.

JONATHAN [*Sadly.*] I know. That's the trouble. You take the time to build a telescope that can sa-see for miles, then there's nothing out there to see. Ma-Mother says it's a lesson in Life. [*Pause.*] But I'm not sorry I built my telescope. And you know why? Because I saw you. Even if I didn't see anything else, I did see you. And . . . and I'm . . . very glad. [ROSALIE *moves slightly closer to him on the couch. She moistens her lips.*] I . . . I remember, you were standing across the way in your penthouse garden playing blind man's buff with ten little children. [*After a short pause, fearfully.*] Are . . . are they by any chance . . . *yours?*

ROSALIE [*Sweetly*]. Oh, I'm not married.

JONATHAN. Oh!

ROSALIE. I'm a baby sitter.

JONATHAN [*With obvious relief*]. Oh.

ROSALIE. I work for the people who own the penthouse.

JONATHAN. I've never seen them around.

ROSALIE. I've never seen them either. They're never home. They just mail me a check every week and tell me to make sure I keep the children's names straight.

JONATHAN. If you could tell me which way they went I could find them with my telescope. It can see for miles.

ROSALIE. They must love children very much. I'll bet she's a marvelous woman. [*Pause.*] There's going to be another one, too! Another child is coming! I got a night letter last night.

JONATHAN. By airplane?

ROSALIE. I don't know.

JONATHAN. I bet it was. I can't see at night. Ma-Mother can but I can't. I'll bet that's when the planes fly.

ROSALIE [*Coyly*]. If you like, I'll read you the letter. I have it with me. [*She unbuttons the top of her blouse and turns around in a coquettish manner to take the letter from her brassiere. Reading.*] "Have had another child. Sent it yesterday. Will arrive tomorrow. Call it Cynthia."

JONATHAN. That will make eleven. That's an awful lot of children to take care of. I'll bet it must be wonderful.

ROSALIE. They do pay very well.

JONATHAN. They pay you?

ROSALIE. Of course . . . What did you think? [*Pause. Softly, seductively.*] Jonathan? [*He does not answer but seems lost in thought. With a feline purr.*] Jonathan?

JONATHAN. Yyyyyes?

ROSALIE. It gets very lonesome over there. The children go to sleep early and the parents are never home so I'm always alone. Perhaps . . . well Jonathan, I thought that perhaps you might . . . visit me.

JONATHAN. Well . . . well . . . well, you . . . you see . . . I . . . I . . .

ROSALIE. We could spend the evenings together . . . at my place. It gets so lonesome there, you know what I mean? I mean, I don't know what to do. I get so lonesome there.

JONATHAN. Ma-ma-ma-maybe you . . . you can . . . come over . . . here? Maybe you you can do . . . that.

ROSALIE. Why are you trembling so?

JONATHAN. I'm . . . I'm . . . I'm . . . I'm . . .

ROSALIE. Are you afraid?

JONATHAN. Nnnnnnnnnnnnnnnnnnnnno. Whaaaaaaaaaa-why . . . should I . . . be . . . afraid?

ROSALIE. Then why won't you come visit me?

JONATHAN. I . . . I . . . I . . . I . . .

ROSALIE. I don't think you're allowed to go out. That's what I think.

JONATHAN. Nnnn-o. I . . . I can . . . can . . . can . . .

ROSALIE. Why can't you go out, Jonathan? I want to know.

JONATHAN. Nnnnnnnnn-

ROSALIE. Tell me, Jonathan!

JONATHAN. I . . . I . . .

ROSALIE. I said I want to know! *Tell me.*

JONATHAN. I . . . I don't . . . know. I don't know why. I mean, I've . . . nnnnnnnever really thought . . . about going out. I . . . guess it's . . . just natural for me to . . . stay inside. [*He laughs nervously as if that explained everything.*] You see . . . I've got so much to do. I mean, all my ssssstamps and . . . ca-coins and books. The pa-pa-plane might fffffly overhead while I was was going downstairs. And then thhhhere are . . . the plants ta-to feeeeeeed. And I enjoy vvvery much wa . . . watching you and all yyyyyyour chil-dren. I've . . . really got so ma-many things . . . to . . . do. Like . . . like my future, for instance. Ma-Mother says I'm going to be great. That's . . . that's . . . that's what she . . . says. I'm going to be great. I ssssswear. Of course, she doesn't know ex-actly what I'm . . . going to be great *in* . . . so she sits every afternoon for . . . for two hours and thinks about it. Na-na-naturally I've . . . got to be here when she's thinking in case she . . . thinks of the answer. Otherwise she might forget and I'd never know . . . what I'm ga-going to be great in. You . . . see what I mean? I mean, I've . . . I've gggggot so many things to do I . . . just couldn't possibly get *anything* done if I ever . . . went . . . out-side. [*There is a silence.* JONATHAN *stares at* ROSALIE *as if he were hoping that might answer her question sufficiently. She stares back at him as if she knows there is more.*] Besides, Mother locks the front door.

ROSALIE. I thought so.

JONATHAN. No! You-you don't understand. It's not what you think. She doesn't lock the door to kaka-keep me in, which would be malicious. She . . . locks the door so I can't get out, which is for my own good and therefore . . . beneficent.

Cuckoo Clock [*From the master bedroom*]. Cuckoo! Cuckoo! Cuckoo!

Rosalie. What's that?

Jonathan [*Fearfully*]. A warning.

Rosalie. What do you mean, a warning?

Jonathan. A warning that you have to go. Your time is up.

Rosalie. My time is what?

Jonathan. Your time is up. You have to go. Now. At once. Right away. You can't stay any longer. You've got to go!

Rosalie. Why?

Jonathan [*Puzzled: as if this were the first time the question had ever occurred to him*]. I don't really know.

Cuckoo Clock [*Louder*]. Cuckoo! Cuckoo! Cuckoo! [Jonathan *freezes in terror.* Rosalie *looks at him calmly.*]

Rosalie. Why did your mother ask me to come up here?

Jonathan. What?

Rosalie. Why did your mother ask me—?

Jonathan. So I . . . I could meet you.

Rosalie. Then why didn't you ask me yourself? Something's wrong around here, Jonathan. I don't understand why you didn't ask me yourself.

JONATHAN. Ma-Mother's so much better at those things.

CUCKOO CLOCK [*Very loudly*]. CUCKOO! CUCKOO! CUCKOO!

JONATHAN. You've got to get out of here! That's the third warning. [*He starts to push her toward the door.*]

ROSALIE. Will you call me on the phone?

JONATHAN. Please, you've got to go!

ROSALIE. Instead of your mother telling me to come, will you come and get me yourself? Will you at least call me? Wave to me?

JONATHAN. Yes-yes—I'll do that. Now get out of here!

ROSALIE. I want you to promise to come and see me again.

JONATHAN. Get out!

ROSALIE [*Coyly*]. Promise me.

JONATHAN. GET OUT! [*He pushes her toward the door.*]

ROSALIE. Why do you keep looking at that door?

JONATHAN [*Almost in tears*]. *Please.*

ROSALIE. Why do you keep looking at that door?

JONATHAN. *Please!* You've got to go before it's too late!

ROSALIE. There's something very wrong here. I want to see what's behind that door. [*She starts toward the master bedroom.* JONATHAN *throws his arms about her legs and collapses at her feet, his face buried against her thighs.*]

JONATHAN [*Sobbing uncontrollably*]. I love you. [ROSALIE *stops dead in her tracks and stares down at Jonathan.*]

ROSALIE. What did you say?

JONATHAN. I-I-I lllllllove you. I love you, I love you, I love you I—
The CUCKOO CLOCK *screams, cackles, and goes out of its mind, its call ending in a crazed, strident rasp as if it had broken all its springs, screws, and innards. The door to the master bedroom opens.* MADAME ROSEPETTLE *appears.*

JONATHAN [*Weakly*]. *Too late.*

MADAME ROSEPETTLE. Two warnings are enough for any man. Three are enough for any woman. The cuckoo struck three times and then a fourth and still she's here. May I ask why?

ROSALIE. You've been listening at the keyhole, haven't you!

MADAME ROSEPETTLE. I'm talking to my son, harlot!

ROSALIE. What did you say!

MADAME ROSEPETTLE. Harlot, I called you! Slut, scum, sleazy prostitute catching and caressing children and men. Stroking their hearts. I've seen you.

ROSALIE. What are you talking about?

MADAME ROSEPETTLE. Blind man's buff with the children in the garden. The redheaded one—fifteen, I think. Behind the bush while the others cover their eyes. Up with the skirt, one-two-three and it's done. Don't try to deny it. I've seen you in action. I know your kind.

ROSALIE. That's a lie!

MADAME ROSEPETTLE. Life is a lie, my sweet. Not words but Life itself. Life in all its ugliness. It builds green trees that tease your eyes and draw you under them. Then when you're there in the shade and you breathe in and say, "Oh God, how beautiful," that's when the bird on the branch lets go his droppings and hits you on the head. Life, my sweet, beware. It isn't what it seems. I've seen what it can do. I've watched you dance.

ROSALIE. What do you mean by that?

MADAME ROSEPETTLE. Don't try to deny it. I've watched you closely and I know what I see. You danced too near him and you let him do too much. I saw you rub your hand across the back of his neck. I saw you laugh and look closely in his eyes. I'll bet you even told him he was the only one. How many, I wonder, have you told that to? I saw you let him stroke you with his hairy paw and saw you smile. I fancy your thighs must have fairly trembled. It was, my dear, obscene, lewd, disgusting, and quite disgraceful. Everyone was staring at you and yet you went right on. Don't try to deny it. Words will only make it worse. It would be best for all concerned if you left at once and never came again. I will keep the story of your dancing quiet. Good day. MADAME ROSEPETTLE *turns to leave.* ROSALIE *does not move.*]

ROSALIE. Why don't you let Jonathan out of his room?

MADAME ROSEPETTLE [*Sharply*]. Who!?

ROSALIE. Jonathan.

MADAME ROSEPETTLE. Who!?

ROSALIE. Your son

MADAME ROSEPETTLE. You mean Albert? Is that who you mean? Albert?

JONATHAN. Pa-pa-please do-don't.

MADAME ROSEPETTLE. Is that who you mean, slut? H'm? Speak up? Is that who you mean?

ROSALIE. I mean your son.

MADAME ROSEPETTLE. *I don't let him out because he is my son.* I don't let him out because his skin is as white as fresh snow and he would burn if the sun struck him. I don't let him out because outside there are trees with birds sitting on their branches waiting for him to walk beneath. I don't let him out because you're there, waiting behind the bushes with your skirt up. I don't let him out because he is *susceptible.* That's why. Because he is *susceptible.* Susceptible to trees and to sluts and to sunstroke.

ROSALIE. Then why did you come and get me?

MADAME ROSEPETTLE. Because, my dear, my stupid son has been watching you through that stupid telescope he made. Because, in short, he wanted to meet you and I, in short, wanted him to know what you were really like. Now that he's seen, you may go.

ROSALIE. And if I choose to stay? [*Pause.*]

MADAME ROSEPETTLE [*Softly: slyly*]. Can you cook?

ROSALIE. Yes.

MADAME ROSEPETTLE. How well?

ROSALIE. Fairly well.

MADAME ROSEPETTLE. Not good enough! My son is a connoisseur. A connoisseur, do you hear? I cook him the finest foods in the world. Recipes no one knows exist. Food, my sweet, is the finest of arts. And since you can't cook you are artless. You nauseate my son's aesthetic taste. Do you like cats?

ROSALIE. Yes.

MADAME ROSEPETTLE. What kind of cats?

ROSALIE. Any kind of cats.

MADAME ROSEPETTLE. Alley cats?

ROSALIE. Especially alley cats.

MADAME ROSEPETTLE. I thought so. Go, my dear. Find yourself some weeping willow and set yourself beneath it. Cry of your lust for my son and wait, for a mocking bird waits above to deposit his verdict on your whorish head. My son is as white as fresh snow and you are tainted with sin. You are garnished with garlic and turn our tender stomachs in disgust.

ROSALIE. What did you come to Havana for?

MADAME ROSEPETTLE. To find *you!*

ROSALIE. And now that you've found me . . . ?

MADAME ROSEPETTLE. I throw you out! I toss you into the garbage can! If you'd have left on time I'd have told the sordid details of your dance when you were gone instead of to your face. But it makes no difference. I heard everything, you know. So don't try to call. The phone is in my room . . . and *no one goes into my room but me.*

She stares at ROSALIE *for a moment, then exits with a flourish.* ROSALIE *and* JONATHAN *move slowly toward each other. When they are almost together* MADAME ROSEPETTLE *reappears.*

One more thing. If, by some chance, the eleventh child named Cynthia turns out to be a Siamese cat, give it to me. I too pay well. [MADAME ROSEPETTLE *turns toward her room.* ROSALIE *starts toward the door.* JONATHAN *grabs her hand in desperation.*]

JONATHAN [*In a whisper*]. Come back again. Pa-please . . .
come back again. [*For a moment* ROSALIE *stops and looks at*
JONATHAN. *But* MADAME ROSEPETTLE *stops too, and turning,
looks back at both of them, a slight smile on her lips.* ROSALIE,
sensing her glance, walks toward the door, slipping from JONA-
THAN's *outstretched hands as she does. The lights fade about*
JONATHAN, *alone in the center of the room.*]

Curtain.

SCENE 3

The hotel room at night, one week later. JONATHAN *is alone in the living room.* He is sitting in a chair near the fish bowl, staring at nothing in particular with a particularly blank expression on his face. A clock is heard ticking softly in the distance. For an interminably long time it continues to tick while JONATHAN sits in his chair, motionless. After a while the ticking speeds up almost imperceptibly and soon after, laughter is heard. At first it is a giggle from the rear of the theater, then a cough from the side, then a self-conscious laugh from the other side, then a full gusty belly-roar from all corners of the theater. Soon the entire world is hysterical. Cuban drums begin to beat. Fireworks explode. Orgiastic music is heard.*

JONATHAN *continues to sit, motionless. Only his eyes have begun to move. The clock continues to tick. The laughter grows louder: the laughter of the insane. Suddenly* JONATHAN *leaps up and rushes to the French windows, his fingers pressed against his ears. He slams the French windows shut. The noises stop.* JONATHAN *closes his eyes and sighs with relief. The French windows sway unsteadily on their hinges. They tip forward. They fall to the floor. They shatter. The laughter returns.*

JONATHAN *stares down at them in horror. The* VENUS'-FLYTRAPS *grow larger and growl.*

VENUS'-FLYTRAPS [*Viciously*]. *Grrrrrr.* [*The* PIRANHA FISH *stares hungrily from its bowl.*]

ROSALINDA THE FISH [*More viciously*]. Grarrgh! [*The* FLYTRAPS *lunge at Jonathan but he walks dazedly past, unaware of their snapping petals, and goes out to the edge of the balcony. He stares out in complete bewilderment. The laughter and music of a carnival, the sounds of people dancing in the streets fill the air. He looks down at them sadly. Meekly he waves. The sounds immediately grow softer and the people begin to drift away. He watches as they leave. Behind him the* FLYTRAPS *keep growing and reaching out for him, but of this he is unaware. He only stands at the railing, looking down. A last lingering laugh is heard somewhere in the distance, echoing.*]
                The door to the suite opens.

FIRST VOICE [*From outside the door*]. Are you sure this is the room?

SECOND VOICE [*Also outside*]. This is the room, all right. [JONATHAN *hides behind one of the* FLYTRAPS *and watches.*]

THIRD VOICE. And she wants all this stuff in here?

FOURTH VOICE. That's what she said.

FIFTH VOICE. Seems strange to me.

SECOND VOICE. Well don't worry about it. Just do it. After all . . . she tips very well.

THIRD VOICE. If you do what she wants.

FOURTH VOICE. Yes. If you do what she wants.

ALL TOGETHER. Well . . . shall we?
They enter. The voices, we discover, belong to the BELLBOYS, *now dressed as waiters. They enter in order.*

BELLBOY NUMBER ONE [*Carrying a small, round table*]. She said to put it here, I think. [*He sets the table down in the center of the room. The lights slowly begin to fade as an overhead spot begins to illuminate the table.*]

BELLBOYS NUMBER TWO AND THREE [*Carrying chairs in their arms*]. And these here. [*They set one chair on either side of the table.*]

BELLBOY NUMBER FOUR [*Carrying an ice bucket with a huge bottle of champagne in it*]. And the champagne here. [*He sets the ice bucket on the floor between the two chairs at the rear of the table.*]

BELLBOY NUMBER TWO. But what about the candles?

BELLBOY NUMBER THREE. And the glasses?

BELLBOY NUMBER FOUR. And the one wilting rose?

Enter BELLBOY NUMBER FIVE *carrying a tray with two champagne glasses on it, two flickering candles, and a flower vase with one wilting rose protruding.*

BELLBOY NUMBER FIVE. I've got them here.

BELLBOY NUMBER ONE [*Placing a tablecloth on the table*]. Then everything is set.

BELLBOY NUMBER TWO. Just the way she wanted it.

BELLBOY NUMBER THREE. *Exactly* the way she wanted it.

BELLBOY NUMBER FIVE. *Specifically* wanted it. [*He finishes setting the glasses, candles, and flower vase.*]

BELLBOY NUMBER ONE. Yes. Everything is set.

BELLBOY NUMBER FOUR. No. Something is missing.

OTHERS. What!

BELLBOY NUMBER FOUR. We have forgotten something.

OTHERS. Forgotten *what?*

BELLBOY NUMBER FOUR. Well, it seems that we have forgotten the— [*He is interrupted by the sound of a Viennese waltz playing softly, romantically in the background.*]

BELLBOY NUMBER ONE. Oh, I'm sorry. I guess I didn't tell you. She said she'd take care of the music herself.

The lights fade in the room and only the table is lit. The BELLBOYS *disappear into the shadows. The music grows in brilliance.* THE COMMODORE *and* MADAME ROSEPETTLE *waltz into the room. A spot of light follows them about the floor.*

THE COMMODORE. How lovely it was this evening, madame, don't you think? [*She laughs softly and demurely and discretely lowers her eyes. They waltz about the floor.*] How gentle the wind was, madame. And the stars, how clear and bright they were, don't you think? [*She blushes with innocence. They dance on.*] And the moon, madame, shining across the water, lighting the yachts, anchored, so silent and white and clean, waiting for the wind to come and fill their great, clean, white sails again. How poetic it was. How pure, madame. How innocent . . . don't you think? [*She turns her face away and smiles softly. They begin to whirl about the floor.*] Ah, the waltz. How exquisite it is, madame, don't you think? One-two-three, one-two-three, one-two-three. Ahhhhh, madame, how classically simple. How mathematically simple. How stark; how strong . . . how romantic . . . how sublime. [*She giggles girlishly. They whirl madly about the floor.*] Oh, if only Madame knew how I've waited for this moment. If only Madame knew how long. How this week, these nights, the nights we shared together on my yacht; the warm, wonderful nights, the almost-perfect nights, the would-have-been-perfect nights had it not been for the crew peeking through the portholes. Ah, those nights, madame, those nights; almost alone but never quite; but now, tonight, at last, we *are* alone. And now, madame, now we are ready for romance. For the night was made for Love. And tonight, madame . . . we will love.

MADAME ROSEPETTLE [*With the blush of innocence*]. Oh, Commodore, how you do talk. [*They whirl about the room as the lilting rhythm of the waltz grows and sweeps on and on.*]

THE COMMODORE [*Suavely*]. Madame, may I kiss you?

MADAME ROSEPETTLE. Why?

THE COMMODORE [*After recovering from the abruptness of the question; with forced suaveness*]. Your lips . . . are a thing of beauty.

MADAME ROSEPETTLE. My lips, Commodore, are the color of blood. [*She smiles at him. He stares blankly ahead. They dance on.*] I must say, you dance exceptionally well . . . for a man your age.

THE COMMODORE [*Bristling*]. I dance with *you*, madame. That is why I dance well. For to dance with you, madame—is to hold you.

MADAME ROSEPETTLE. Well, I don't mind your holding me, Commodore, but at the moment you happen to be holding me too tight.

THE COMMODORE. I hold you too dear to hold you too tight, madame. I hold you close, that is all. And I hold you close in the hope that my heart may feel your heart beating.

MADAME ROSEPETTLE. *One*-two-three, *one*-two-three. You're not paying enough attention to the music, Commodore. I'm afraid you've fallen out of step.

THE COMMODORE. Then lead me, madame. Take my hand and lead me wherever you wish. For I would much rather think of my words than my feet.

MADAME ROSEPETTLE [*With great sweetness*]. Why certainly, Commodore. Certainly. If that is what you want . . . it will be my pleasure to oblige. [*They switch hands and she begins to lead him about the floor. They whirl wildly about, spinning faster than they had when* THE COMMODORE *led.*]

MADAME ROSEPETTLE. Beautiful, isn't it, Commodore? The waltz. The Dance of Lovers. I'm so glad you enjoy it so much. [*With a gay laugh she whirls him around the floor. Suddenly he puts his arms about her shoulders and leans close to kiss her. She pulls back.*] Commodore! You were supposed to spin just then. When I squeeze you in the side it means *spin!*

THE COMMODORE [*Flustered*]. I . . . I thought it was a sign of affection. [*She laughs*].

MADAME ROSEPETTLE. You'll learn. [*She squeezes him in the side. He spins about under her arm.*] Ah, you're learning. [*He continues to spin around and around, faster and faster like a runaway top while* MADAME ROSEPETTLE, *not spinning at all, leads him about the floor, a wild smile of ecstasy spreading over her face.*]

THE COMMODORE. Ho-ho, ho-ho. Stop. I'm dizzy. Dizzy. Stop, please. Stop. Ho-ho. Stop. Dizzy. Ho-ho. Stop. Too fast. Slow. Slower. Stop. Ho-ho. Dizzy. Too dizzy. Weeeeeee! [*And then, without any warning at all, she grabs him in the middle of a spin and kisses him. Her back is to the audience, so* THE COMMODORE's *face is visible. At first he is too dizzy to realize that his motion has been stopped. But shortly he does, and his first expression is that of shock. But the kiss is long and the shock turns into perplexity and then, finally, into panic; into fear. He struggles desperately and breaks free from her arms, gasping wildly for air. He points weakly to his chest.*]

THE COMMODORE [*Gasping*]. Asthma. [*His chest heaves as he gulps in air.*] Couldn't breathe. Lungs bad. Asthmatic. Nose stuffed, too. Sinus condition. Couldn't get any air. [*He gasps for air. She starts to walk toward him, slowly.*] Couldn't get any . . . air. [*She nears him. Instinctively he backs away.*] You . . . you surprised me . . . you know. Out . . . of breath. Wasn't . . . ready for that. Didn't . . . expect you to kiss me.

MADAME ROSEPETTLE. I know. That's why I did it. [*She laughs and puts her arm tenderly about his waist.*] Perhaps you'd prefer to sit down for a while, Commodore. Catch your breath, so to speak. Dancing can be so terribly tiring . . . when you're growing old. Well, if you like, Commodore, we could just sit and talk. And perhaps . . . sip some pink champagne, eh? Champagne?

THE COMMODORE. Ah, champagne. [*She begins to walk with him toward the table.*]

MADAME ROSEPETTLE. And just for the two of us.

THE COMMODORE. Yes. The two of us. Alone.

MADAME ROSEPETTLE [*With a laugh*]. Yes. All alone.

THE COMMODORE. At last.

MADAME ROSEPETTLE. With music in the distance.

THE COMMODORE. A waltz.

MADAME ROSEPETTLE. A *Viennese* waltz.

THE COMMODORE. The Dance of Lovers. [*She takes his hand, tenderly.*]

MADAME ROSEPETTLE. Yes, Commodore. The Dance of Lovers. [*They look at each other in silence.*]

THE COMMODORE. Madame, you have won my heart. And easily.

MADAME ROSEPETTLE. No, Commodore. You have lost it. *Easily.* [*She smiles seductively. The room darkens till only a single spot of light falls upon the table set in the middle of the room. The waltz plays on.* MADAME ROSEPETTLE *nods to* THE COMMODORE *and he goes to sit. But before he can pull his chair out, it slides out under its own power. He places himself and the chair slides back in, as if some invisible waiter had been holding it in his invisible hands.* MADAME ROSEPETTLE *smiles sweetly and, pulling out her chair herself, sits. They stare at each other in silence. The waltz plays softly.* THE COMMODORE *reaches across the table and touches her hand. A thin smile spreads across her lips. When finally they speak, their words are soft: the whispered thoughts of lovers.*]

MADAME ROSEPETTLE. Champagne?

THE COMMODORE. Champagne.

MADAME ROSEPETTLE. Pour?

THE COMMODORE. Please. [*She lifts the bottle out of the ice bucket and pours with her right hand, her left being clasped firmly in* THE COMMODORE's *passionate hands. They smile serenely at each other. She lifts her glass. He lifts his. The music swells.*]

MADAME ROSEPETTLE. A toast?

THE COMMODORE. To you.

MADAME ROSEPETTLE. No, Commodore, to you.

THE COMMODORE. No, madame. To us.

MADAME ROSEPETTLE⎫ [*Together*]. To us. [*They raise their*
THE COMMODORE   ⎭
*glasses. They gaze wistfully into each other's eyes. The music
builds to brilliance.* THE COMMODORE *clinks his glass against*
MADAME ROSEPETTLE'S *glass. The glasses break.*]

THE COMMODORE [*Furiously mopping up the mess.*] Pardon,
madame! Pardon!

MADAME ROSEPETTLE [*Flicking some glass off her bodice*]. Pas
de quoi, monsieur.

THE COMMODORE. J'étais emporté par l'enthousiasme du moment.

MADAME ROSEPETTLE [*Extracting pieces of glass from her lap*].
Pas de quoi. [THE COMMODORE *suddenly stretches across the table
in order to stop the puddle of champagne from spilling over onto*
MADAME ROSEPETTLE'S *glass-spattered lap. His elbow knocks over
the flower vase. The table is inundated with water.*]

THE COMMODORE [*Gasping*]. Mon dieu!

MADAME ROSEPETTLE [*Watching with a serenely inane grin, as
the water pours over the edge of the table and onto her dress*].
Pas de quoi, monsieur. Pas de quoi.

She snaps her fingers gaily. Immediately a WAITER *appears from
the shadow with a table in his hands. It is already covered with
a tablecloth, two champagne glasses, two candelabra (the candles
already flickering in them), and a vase with one wilting rose protruding. Another* WAITER *whisks the wet table away. The new
table is placed. The* WAITERS *disappear into the shadows.*

MADAME ROSEPETTLE [*Lifting the bottle of champagne out of
the ice bucket*]. Encore?

THE COMMODORE. S'il vous plaît. [*She pours. They lift their glasses in a toast. The music swells again.*] To us.

MADAME ROSEPETTLE. To us, monsieur . . . Commodore. [*They clink their glasses lightly.* THE COMMODORE *closes his eyes and sips.* MADAME ROSEPETTLE *holds her glass before her lips, poised but not touching, waiting. She watches him. Then she speaks softly.*] Tell me about yourself.

THE COMMODORE. My heart is speaking, madame. Doesn't it tell you enough?

MADAME ROSEPETTLE. Your heart, monsieur, is growing old. It speaks with a murmur. Its words are too weak to understand.

THE COMMODORE. But the feeling, madame, is still strong.

MADAME ROSEPETTLE. Feelings are for animals, monsieur. Words are the specialty of Man. Tell me what your heart has to say.

THE COMMODORE. My heart says it loves you.

MADAME ROSEPETTLE. And how many others, monsieur, has your heart said this to?

THE COMMODORE. None but you, madame. None but you.

MADAME ROSEPETTLE. And you, monsieur, with all your money and your worldly ways, how many have loved you?

THE COMMODORE. Many, madame.

MADAME ROSEPETTLE. How many, monsieur?

THE COMMODORE. Too many, madame

MADAME ROSEPETTLE. So I, alone, am different?

THE COMMODORE. You alone . . . do I love.

MADAME ROSEPETTLE. And pray, monsieur, just what is it that I've done to make you love me so?

THE COMMODORE. Nothing, madame. And that is why. You are a strange woman, you see. You go out with me and you know how I feel. Yet, I know nothing of you. You disregard me, madame, but never discourage. You treat my love with indifference . . . but never disdain. You've led me on, madame. That is what I mean to say.

MADAME ROSEPETTLE. I've led you to my room, monsieur. That is all.

THE COMMODORE. To me, that is enough.

MADAME ROSEPETTLE. I know. That's why I did it. [*The music swells. She smiles distantly. There is a momentary silence.*]

THE COMMODORE [*With desperation*]. Madame, I must ask you something. Now. Because in all the days I've been with you there's been something I've wanted to know, but you've never told me so now, right now, I must ask. Madame, why are you here?

MADAME ROSEPETTLE [*She pauses before answering*]. I have to be somewhere, don't I?

THE COMMODORE. But why here, where I am? Why in Havana?

MADAME ROSEPETTLE. You flatter yourself, monsieur. I am in Havana only because Havana was in my way. . . . I think I'll move on tomorrow.

THE COMMODORE. For . . . home?

MADAME ROSEPETTLE [*Laughing slightly*]. Only the very young and the very old have homes. I am neither. And I have none.

THE COMMODORE. But . . . surely you must come from somewhere.

MADAME ROSEPETTLE. Nowhere you've ever been.

THE COMMODORE. I've been many places.

MADAME ROSEPETTLE [*Softly*]. But not many enough. [*She picks up her glass of champagne and sips, a distant smile on her lips.*]

THE COMMODORE [*With sudden, overwhelming, and soul-rendering passion*]. Madame, don't go tomorrow. Stay. My heart is yours.

MADAME ROSEPETTLE. How much is it worth?

THE COMMODORE. A fortune, madame.

MADAME ROSEPETTLE. Good. I'll take it in cash.

THE COMMODORE. But the heart goes with it, madame.

MADAME ROSEPETTLE. And you with the heart, I suppose?

THE COMMODORE. Forever.

MADAME ROSEPETTLE. Sorry, monsieur. The money's enticing and the heart would have been nice, but you, I'm afraid, are a bit too bulky to make it all worth while.

THE COMMODORE. You jest, madame.

MADAME ROSEPETTLE. I never jest, monsieur. There isn't enough time.

THE COMMODORE. Then you make fun of my passion, madame, which is just as bad.

MADAME ROSEPETTLE. But monsieur, I've never taken your passion seriously enough to make fun of it. [*There is a short pause.* THE COMMODORE *sinks slowly back in his seat.*]

THE COMMODORE [*Weakly, sadly*]. Then why have you gone out with me?

MADAME ROSEPETTLE. So that I might drink champagne with you tonight.

THE COMMODORE. That makes no sense.

MADAME ROSEPETTLE. It makes *perfect* sense.

THE COMMODORE. Not to me.

MADAME ROSEPETTLE. It does to me.

THE COMMODORE. But *I* don't understand. And I *want* to understand.

MADAME ROSEPETTLE. Don't worry, Commodore. You will.

THE COMMODORE. When?

MADAME ROSEPETTLE. Soon.

THE COMMODORE. How soon?

MADAME ROSEPETTLE. Very soon. [*He stares at her in submissive confusion. Suddenly, with final desperation, he grabs her hands in his and, leaning across the table, kisses them passionately, sobbingly. Then in a scarcely audible whisper she says.*] Now.

THE COMMODORE. Madame . . . I love you. Forever. Don't you understand? [*He kisses her hand again. A smile of triumph spreads across her face.*] Oh, your husband . . . He must have been . . . a wonderful man . . . to deserve a woman such as you. [*He sobs and kisses her hands again.*]

MADAME ROSEPETTLE [*Nonchalantly*]. Would you like to see him?

THE COMMODORE. A snapshot?

MADAME ROSEPETTLE. No. My husband. He's inside in the closet. I had him stuffed. Wonderful taxidermist I know. H'm? What do you say, Commodore? Wanna peek? He's my very favorite trophy. I take him with me wherever I go.

THE COMMODORE [*Shaken; not knowing what to make of it*]. Hah-hah, hah-hah. Yes. Very good. Very funny. Sort of a . . . um . . . *white elephant*, you might say.

MADAME ROSEPETTLE. *You* might say.

THE COMMODORE. Well, it's . . . certainly very . . . courageous of you, a . . . a woman still in mourning, to . . . to be able to laugh at what most other women wouldn't find . . . well, shall we say . . . funny.

MADAME ROSEPETTLE. Life, my dear Commodore, is *never* funny. It's grim! It's there every morning breathing in your face the moment you open your red baggy eyes. Worst of all, it follows you wherever you go. Life, Mr. Roseabove, is a husband hanging from a hook in the closet. Open the door without your customary cup of coffee and your whole day's shot to hell. But open the door just a little ways, sneak your hand in, pull out your dress, and your day is made. Yet he's still there, and waiting—your husband, hanging by his collar from a hook, and sooner or later the moth balls are gone and you've got to clean house. It's a bad day, Commodore, when you have to stare Life in the face, and you find he doesn't smile at all; just hangs there . . . with his tongue sticking out.

THE COMMODORE. I . . don't find this . . . very funny.

MADAME ROSEPETTLE. Sorry. I was hoping it would give you a laugh.

THE COMMODORE. I don't think it's funny at all. And the reason that I don't think it's funny at all is that it's not my kind of joke. One must respect the dead.

MADAME ROSEPETTLE. Then tell me, Commodore . . . why not the living, too? [*Pause. She lifts out the bottle of champagne and pours herself some more.*]

THE COMMODORE [*Weakly, with a trace of fear*]. How . . . how did he die?

MADAME ROSEPETTLE. Why, I killed him of course. Champagne? [*She smiles sweetly and fills his glass. She raises hers in a toast.*] To your continued good health. [*He stares at her blankly. The music swells in the background.*] Ah, the waltz, monsieur. Listen. The waltz. The Dance of Lovers. Beautiful . . . *don't you think?* [*She laughs and sips some more champagne. The music grows to brilliance.* THE COMMODORE *starts to rise from his chair.*]

THE COMMODORE. Forgive me, madame. But . . . I find I must leave. Urgent business calls. Good evening. [*He tries to push his chair back, but for some reason it will not move. He looks about in panic. He pushes frantically. It does not move. It is as if the invisible waiter who had come and slid the chair out when he went to sit down now stood behind the chair and held it in so*

he could not get up. And as there are arms on the chair, THE
COMMODORE *cannot slide out the side.* MADAME ROSEPETTLE
smiles.]

MADAME ROSEPETTLE. Now you don't *really* want to leave . . .
do you, Commodore? After all, the night is still so young . . .
and you haven't even seen my husband yet. We shared such love
for so many years, Commodore, I would so regret if you had to
leave without seeing him. And believe me, Commodore, the
expression on his face is easily worth the price of admission. So
please, Commodore, won't you reconsider? Won't you stay? . . .
just for a little while? [*He stares at her in horror. He tries once
more to push his chair back. But the chair does not move. He
sinks down into it weakly. She leans across the table and tenderly
touches his hand.*] Good. I knew you'd see it my way. It would
have been such a shame if you'd have had to leave. For you see,
Commodore, we are in a way united. We share something in
common . . . you and I. . . . We share desire. For you desire
me, with love in your heart. While I, my dear Commodore . . .
desire your heart. [*She smiles sweetly and sips some more champagne.*] How simple it all is, in the end. [*She rises slowly from
her chair and walks over to him. She runs her hands lovingly
through his hair and down the back of his neck.*] Tell me, Commodore, how would you like to hear a little story? A bedtime story?
A fairy tale full of handsome princes and enchanted maidens;
full of love and joy and music; tenderness and charm? Would
you like to hear it, Commodore? Eh? It's my very favorite story,
you see . . . and since you're my very favorite commodore, it
seems only appropriate that I tell it to you . . . *don't you think?*

THE COMMODORE. No. I . . . I don't think so.

MADAME ROSEPETTLE. Good. Then I'll tell it. I never leave a
place without telling it to at least one person. How very lucky you
are. How very lucky. [*The light on the table dims slightly*

MADAME ROSEPETTLE *walks slowly away. A spot of light follows her as she goes. The light on the table fades more.* THE COMMODORE *sits, motionless.*]
His name was Albert Edward Robinson Rosepettle III. How strange and sad he was. All the others who had come to see me had been tall, but he was short. They had been rich, while he was poor. The others had been handsome, but Albert, poor Albert, he was as ugly as a humid day . . . [*She laughs sadly, distantly.*] and just about as wet, too. Oh, he was a fat bundle of sweat, Mr. Roseabove. He was nothing but one great torrent of perspiration. Winter and summer, spring and fall, Albert was dripping wet. And he wasn't very good-looking either. He had a large green wart on the very tip of his nose and he talked with a lisp and walked with a limp and his left ear, which was slightly larger than his right, was as red as a bright red beet. He was round and wet and hideous and I never could figure out how he ever got such a name as Albert Edward Robinson Rosepettle III.
Oh, I must have been very susceptible indeed to have married Albert. I *was* twenty-eight and that *is* a susceptible year in a woman's life. And of course I *was* a virgin, but still I— Oh, stop blushing, Mr. Roseabove. I'm not lying. It's all true. Part of the cause of my condition, I will admit, was due to the fact that I still hadn't gone out with a man. But I am certain, Mr. Roseabove, I am certain that despite your naughty glances my virtue would have remained unsoiled, no matter what. Oh, I had spoken to men. (Their voices are gruff.) And in crowded streets I had often brushed against them. (Their bodies, I found, are tough and bony.) I had observed their ways and habits, Mr. Roseabove. Even at that tender age I had the foresight to realize I must know what I was up against. So I watched them huddled in hallways, talking in nervous whispers and laughing when little girls passed by. I watched their hands in crowded buses and even felt their feeling elbows on crowded streets. And then, one night, when I was walking home I saw a man standing in a window. I saw him take his contact lenses out and his hearing aid out of his ear. I saw him take his teeth out of his thin-lipped mouth and drop

them into a smiling glass of water. I saw him lift his snow-white hair off of his wrinkled white head and place it on a gnarled wooden hat tree. And then I saw him take his clothes off. And when he was done and didn't move but stood and stared at a full-length mirror whose glass he had covered with towels, then I went home and wept.

And so one day I bolted the door to my room. I locked myself inside, bought a small revolver just in case, then sat at my window and watched what went on below. It was not a pretty sight. Some men came up to see me. I don't know how they got my name. But I have heard that once a woman reaches womanhood her fragrance wanders out into the world and her name becomes the common property of Men. Just as a single drop of blood will attract a distant school of sharks, so Man, without any introduction, can catch the scent of any woman anywhere and find her home. That is what I've heard. No place then is safe from them. You cannot hide. Your name is known and there is nothing left that can be done. I suppose if you like you can lock your door. It doesn't keep them away; just keeps them out. I locked my door. They came and knocked. I did not let them in.

"Hello in there," they said.

"Hello in there,
My name is Steven.
Steven S. (for Steven) Steven.
One is odd
But two is even.
I know you're hot
So I'm not leavin'."

. . . or something like that.

[*Short pause.*] But they all soon left anyway. I think they caught the scent of a younger woman down the hall. And so I stayed inside my room and listened to the constant sound of feet disappearing down the stairs. I watched a world walk by my window; a world of lechery and lies and greed. I watched a world walk by and I decided not to leave my room until this world came to me, *exactly* as I wanted it.

One day Albert came toddling up the stairs. He waddled over
to my room, scratched on the door and said, in a frail and very
frightened voice, "Will you please marry me?" And so I did.
It was as simple as that. [*Pause. Then distantly.*] I still wonder
why I did it though. I still wonder why. [*Short pause.Then with a
laugh of resignation.*] I don't really know why. I guess it just
seemed like the right thing to do. Maybe it's because he was the
first one who ever asked me. No, that's not right. . . . Perhaps
it's because he was so ugly and fat; so unlike everything I'd ever
heard a husband should be. No, that doesn't make much sense
either. . . . Perhaps it's . . . yes, perhaps it's because one look
at Albert's round, sad face and I knew he could be mine . . . that
no matter where he went, or whom he saw, or what he did, Albert
would be mine, all mine—mine to love, mine to live with, mine
to kill; my husband, my lover, my own . . . *my very own.*
And so we were wed. That night I went to bed with a man
for the first time in my life. The next morning I picked up my
mattress and moved myself into another room. Not that there
was something wrong with Albert. Oh, no! He was *quite* the
picture of health. His pudgy, pink flesh bouncing with glee. Oh,
how easily is Man satisfied. How easily is his porous body
saturated with "fun." All he asks is a little sex and a little food
and there he is, asleep with a smile and snoring. Never the slightest
regard for you, lying in bed next to him, your eyes open wide.
No, he stretches his legs and kicks you in the shins; stretches his
arms and smacks you in the eye. Lean over to kiss him good night
and he'll belch in your face till all your romantic dreams are
dissolved in an image of onions, garlic, and baked Boston beans.
Oh, how considerate is Man when he's had his fill of sex. How
noble, how magical, how marvelous is Love.
And so, I picked up my mattress and left his room. For as long
as I stayed in his room I was not safe. After all, he was a total
stranger to me. We'd only met the day before and I knew far
too little. But now that we were married I had time to find out
more. His life was a mystery and his mind contained too many
secrets. In short, I was in danger. So I decided to find out certain

things. A few of these were: what had he done before we'd ever met, what had he wanted to do, what did he still want to do, what was he doing about it? What did he dream about while he slept? What did he think about when he stared out the window? What did he think about when I wasn't near?

These were the things that concerned me most. And so I began to watch him closely.

My plan worked best at night, for that was when he slept. . . . I would listen at my door until I heard his door close. Then I'd tiptoe out and watch him through his keyhole. When his lights went out I'd open up his door and creep across the floor to his bed. And that, Mr. Roseabove, is where I stayed, every night— next to him; my husband, my "Love." I never left his side, never took my eyes from his sleeping face. I dare you to find me a wife who's as devoted as that. [*She laughs.*] And so I watched. I listened to him breathe. My ear was a stethoscope that recorded the fluctuations of his dream life. I put my ear next to his mouth so I might hear the slightest word that he might say, the slightest word that would betray his sleeping, secret thoughts. I listened for my name upon his lips. I listened for a word of "love." I listened for anything, but he only snored, and smiled, and slept on and on. So every night I waited and listened, and every morning when the dawn came I left, knowing no more than when I'd come.

A month later I found that I was pregnant. It had happened that first horrible night. How like Albert to do something like that. I fancy he knew it was going to happen all the time, too. I do believe he planned it that way. One night, one shot, one chance in a lifetime and bham! you've had it. It takes an imaginative man to miss. It takes someone like Albert to do something like that. But yet, I never let on. Oh, no. Let him think I'm simply getting fat, I said. And that's the way I did it, too. I, nonchalantly putting on weight; Albert nonchalantly watching my belly grow. If he knew what was happening to me he never let me know it. He was as silent as before. It was only at night that he changed. Only at night while he slept that something strange suddenly occurred. I found that the smile on his face had become a grin. [*Pause.*]

Twelve months later my son was born. He was so overdue that when he came out he was already teething. He bit the index finger off the poor doctor's hand and snapped at the nurse till she fainted. I took him home and put him in a cage in the darkest corner of my room. But still I—

THE COMMODORE. Was it a large cage?

MADAME ROSEPETTLE. What?

THE COMMODORE. Was his cage large? I hope it was. Otherwise it wouldn't be very comfortable.

MADAME ROSEPETTLE. I'm sorry. Did I say cage? I meant crib. I put him in a crib and set the crib in a corner of my room where my husband would not see him. For until I found out exactly why he'd married me, until I understood his dreams, until that time I was not safe, and until that time I would not tell him that his son had been born. And so I went on as if nothing had happened. At night I'd slip into his room and watch him while he slept. He still refused to say a word. And yet, somehow, his grin seemed broader. And then, one night, he made that noise. At first I thought it just some . . . sort of snore. But then I listened closely. I was wrong. I know it sounds peculiar, Mr. Roseabove, but I swear it's true. While I looked on, Albert slept . . . and giggled. [*Pause.*]

Shortly after that, Rosalinda came. She was one of Albert's many secretaries. Since I'd married him, you see, he'd become a multibillionaire. My influence, of course. We'd moved from a four-room flat to a four-acre mansion. Albert had taken the north wing, my son and I the south. But when Rosalinda came, things changed. I've always felt there was something star-crossed about those two, for she was the only person I ever met who was equally as ugly as he. It seems her mother had once owned a

laundromat and, at the tender age of five, Rosalinda, a curious
child, had taken an exploratory trip through the mangler. The
result of the trip being that her figure took on an uncanny
resemblance to nothing less than a question mark.

Well, naturally I never let on that I knew she had come. When
she walked in front of me I looked straight through her. When
she spoke I looked away. I flatly refused to recognize her presence. I simply set an extra place at the table and cooked a little
bit more. Though Albert watched me like a naughty boy anxious
to see his mother's reaction to a mischievous deed, I disregarded
his indiscretions and continued my life as if nothing had
changed. If he were searching for some sign of annoyance, I never
showed it. If he were waiting to be scolded *I* was waiting for him
to give up. So at night, instead of preparing one, I prepared two
beds. Instead of fluffing one pillow I fluffed up two and straightened
an extra pair of sheets. I said good night as politely as I could and
left them alone—the hunchback and my husband, two soulmates
expressing their souls through sin. And while they lay in bed I
listened at the keyhole. And when they slept I crept in and
listened more. Albert had begun to speak!

After months of listening for some meager clue he suddenly
began to talk in torrents. Words poured forth and I, like some
listening sponge, soaked them up and stayed for more. At last he
was talking in his sleep and I was there, sinking farther and
farther into his brain, gaining more and more control. He told
her things he never told to me. Words of passion and love. He
told her how he worshiped the way she cooked; how he worshiped the way she talked; how he'd worshiped the way she'd
looked when he'd first met her; even the way she looked now.
And this to a hunchback. A hunchback! To a hideous, twisted slut
sleeping in sin with him! Words he never told to me. I ask you,
Mr. Roseabove, how much is a woman supposed to take?

But the signs of regret were beginning to show. And oh, how
I laughed when I found out: when I saw how tired he'd begun
to look, when I noticed how little he ate; how little he spoke;
how slowly he seemed to move. It's funny, but he never slept
any more. I could tell by his breathing. And through the keyhole

at night I could see his large, round, empty eyes shining sadly in the dark. [*Pause.*]

Then one night he died. One year after she had come he passed on. The doctors don't know why. His heart, they said, seemed fine. It was as large a heart as they'd ever seen. And yet he died. At one o'clock in the morning his heart stopped beating. [*She laughs softly.*] But it wasn't till dawn that she discovered he was dead. [*She starts to laugh louder.*]

Well, don't you get it? Don't you catch the irony, the joke? What's wrong with you!? He died at one. At ONE O'CLOCK IN THE MORNING!! DEAD!!! Yet she didn't know he was dead till dawn. [*She laughs again, loudly.*]

Well don't you get the point? The point of this whole story? What is wrong with you? He was lying with her in bed for nearly six hours, *dead,* and she never knew it! What a lover he must have been! WHAT A LOVER! [*She laughs uproariously but stops when she realizes he's not laughing with her.*]

Well don't you see? Their affair, their sinfulness—it never even existed! He tried to make me jealous but there was nothing to be jealous of. His love was sterile! He was a child. He was weak. He was impotent. He was *mine!* Mine all the time, even when he was in bed with another, even in death . . . *he was mine!* [THE COMMODORE *climbs up in his chair and crawls over his arm rest. He begins to walk weakly toward the door.*] Don't tell me you're leaving, Commodore. Is there something wrong? [THE COMMODORE *walks weakly toward the door, then runs the last part of the way. In panic he twists the doorknob. The doorknob comes off. He falls to the ground.*] Why Commodore, you're on your knees! *How romantic.* Don't tell me you're going to ask me to marry you again? Commodore, you're trembling. What's wrong? Don't tell me you're afraid that I'll accept?

THE COMMODORE [*Weakly*]. I . . . I-I . . . feel . . . sa-sorry for your . . . ssssson . . . that's . . . all I can . . . sssssay.

MADAME ROSEPETTLE. And I feel sorrier for you! For you are *nothing!* While my son is mine. His skin is the color of fresh

snow, his voice is like the music of angels, and his mind is pure.
For he is safe, Mr. Roseabove, and it is *I* who have saved him.
Saved him from the world beyond that door. The world of you.
The world of his father. A world waiting to devour those who
trust in it; those who love. A world vicious under the hypocrisy of
kindness, ruthless under the falseness of a smile. Well, go on,
Mr. Roseabove. Leave my room and enter your world again—
your sex-driven, dirt-washed waste of cannibals eating each other
up while they pretend they're kissing. Go, Mr. Roseabove, enter
your blind world of darkness. My son shall have only light! [*She
turns with a flourish and enters her bedroom.* THE COMMODORE
*stares helplessly at the doorknob in his hand. Suddenly the door
swings open, under its own power.* THE COMMODORE *crawls out.
The door closes behind him, under its own power. From outside
can be heard the sound of a church bell chiming. The bedroom
door reopens and* MADAME ROSEPETTLE *emerges wearing an immense straw hat, sunglasses, tight toreador pants, and a short
beach robe. She carries a huge flashlight. She is barefoot. She
tiptoes across the floor and exits through the main door. The
church bell chimes thirteen times.*]

JONATHAN *emerges from behind the* VENUS'-FLYTRAPS. *He runs
to the door, puts his ear to it, then races back to the balcony and
stares down at the street below. Carnival lights flash weirdly
against the night sky and laughter drifts up. The* VENUS'-FLYTRAPS
*reach out to grab him but somehow he senses their presence and
leaps away in time.*

VENUS'-FLYTRAPS [*Gruffly*]. Grrrrrrr! [*He walks dazedly into the
living room.*]

ROSALINDA THE FISH. [*Snarlingly*]. Snarrrrrrr! [*The* VENUS'-
FLYTRAPS *have grown enormous. Their monstrous petals wave
hungrily in the air while they growl.* JONATHAN *stares at them
fearfully, the laughter below growing stronger all the while.
Suddenly he runs to the wall and smashes the glass case that
covers the fire axe. He takes out the axe. He advances cautiously
toward the* FLYTRAPS. *He feints an attack, they follow his move-*

ments. *He bobs, they weave. It is a cat-and-mouse game of death. Suddenly* JONATHAN *leaps upon them and hacks them apart till they fall to the floor, writhing, then dead.* JONATHAN *stands above them, victorious, panting, but somehow seeming to breathe easier. Slowly he turns and looks at the fish bowl. His eyes seem glazed, his expression insanely determined. He walks slowly toward the fish bowl. . . . There are three knocks on the door. He does not hear them. He raises his axe.*]

The door opens. ROSALIE *enters. She is dressed in an absurdly childish pink dress with crinolines and frills—the picture of innocence, the picture of a girl ten years old. Her shoes are black leather pumps and she wears short girlish-pink socks. Her cheeks have round circles of rouge on them—like a young girl might have who had never put on make-up before.*

ROSALIE. Jonathan! Jonathan! What *have* you done? [JONATHAN *stops. He does not look at her but stares at the fish bowl.*] Jonathan! Put down that silly axe. You might hurt yourself. [*He still does not answer but stares at the bowl. He does not lower the axe.*] Jonathan! [*Slowly he turns and faces her.*]

JONATHAN. I killed it.

ROSALIE. Ssh. Not so loudly. Where'd you put her body?

JONATHAN [*Pointing to the* PLANTS]. There.

ROSALIE. Where? I don't see a body. Where is she?

JONATHAN. Who?

ROSALIE. Your mother.

JONATHAN. I haven't killed my mother. I've killed her plants. The ones I used to feed. I've chopped their hearts out.

ROSALIE [*With an apologetic laugh*]. I thought you'd . . .

killed your mother. [The PIRANHA FISH *giggles*. JONATHAN *turns and stares at it again. He starts to move toward it, slowly.*]

ROSALIE. Jonathan, stop. [*He hesitates, as if he is uncertain what to do. Slowly he raises the axe.*] Jonathan! [*He smashes the axe against the fish bowl. It breaks. The fish screams.*]

ROSALINDA THE FISH [*Fearfully*]. AAIEEEEEEEEEEEEEEE!

ROSALIE. Now look at the mess you've made.

JONATHAN. Do you think it can live without water?

ROSALIE. What will your mother say when she gets back?

JONATHAN. Maybe I should hit it again. Just in case. [*He strikes it again.*]

ROSALINDA THE FISH [*Mournfully*]. UGHHHHHHH! [JONATHAN *stares in horror at the dead* FISH. *He drops the axe and turns away, sickened and weak.* ROSALIE *walks over and touches him gently, consolingly, on the arm.*]

ROSALIE. There's something bothering you, isn't there? [*Pause —coyly.*] What's-a matter, Jonathan? [JONATHAN *does not answer at first but stares off into space frightened, bewildered.*]

JONATHAN [*Weakly*]. I never thought I'd see you again. I never thought I'd talk to you again. I never thought you'd come.

ROSALIE. Did you really think that?

JONATHAN. She told me she'd never let you visit me again. She said no one would *ever* visit me again. She told me I had seen enough.

ROSALIE. But I had a key made.

JONATHAN. She . . . she hates me.

ROSALIE. What?

JONATHAN. She doesn't let me do anything. She doesn't let me listen to the radio. She took the tube out of the television set. She doesn't let me use her phone. She makes me show her all my letters before I seal them. She doesn't—

ROSALIE. Letters? What letters are you talking about?

JONATHAN. Just . . . letters I write.

ROSALIE. To *whom?*

JONATHAN. To people.

ROSALIE. *What* people?

JONATHAN. Oh . . . various people.

ROSALIE. Other girls? Could they be to other girls, by any chance?

JONATHAN. No. They're just to people. No people in particular. Just people in the phone book. Just names. I do it alphabetically. That way, someday, I'll be able to cover everyone. So far I've covered all the "A's" and "B's" up to Barrera.

ROSALIE. What is it you say to them? Can you tell me what you say to them . . . or is it private? Jonathan, just what do you say to them!?

JONATHAN. Mostly I just ask them what they look like. [*Pause. Suddenly he starts to sob in a curious combination of laughter and tears.*] But I don't think she ever mails them. She reads them, then takes them out to mail. But I don't think she ever does. I'll bet she just throws them away. Well if she's not going to mail them, why does she say she will? I . . . I could save the stamps. Why must she lie to me? Why doesn't she just say she's not going to mail them? Then I wouldn't have to wait for letters every day.

ROSALIE. Guess why I had this key made.

JONATHAN. I'll bet she's never even mailed one. From Abandono to Barrera, not one.

ROSALIE. Do you know why I had this key made? Do you know why I'm wearing this new dress?

JONATHAN. She doesn't let me stand in the window at noon because the sun is too strong. She doesn't let me stand in the window at night when the wind is blowing because the air is too cold. And today she told me she's going to nail shutters over the windows so I'll never have to worry about being bothered by the sun or the wind again.

ROSALIE. Try and guess why I'm all dressed up.

JONATHAN. She tells me I'm brilliant. She makes me read and reread books no one's ever read. She smothers me with blankets at night in case of a storm. She tucks me in so tight I can't even get out till she comes and takes my blankets off.

ROSALIE. Stop talking about that and pay attention to me!

JONATHAN. She says she loves me. Every morning, before I even have a chance to open my eyes, there she is, leaning over my bed, breathing in my face and saying, "I love you, I love you."

ROSALIE. Jonathan, isn't my dress pretty?

JONATHAN. But I heard everything tonight. I heard it all when she didn't know I was here. [He stares off into space, bewildered.]

ROSALIE. What's the matter? [*He does not answer.*] Jonathan, what's the matter?

JONATHAN. But she must have known I was here. She *must* have known! I mean . . . where could I have gone? (*Pause.*) But . . . if that's the case . . . *why did she let me hear?*

ROSALIE. Jonathan, I do wish you'd pay more attention to me. Here, look at my dress. You can even touch it if you like. Guess how many crinolines I have on. Guess why I'm wearing such a pretty, new dress. *Jonathan!*

JONATHAN [*Distantly*]. Maybe . . . it didn't make any difference to her . . . whether I heard or not. [*He turns suddenly to her and hugs her closely. She lets him hold her, then she steps back and away from him. Her face looks strangely old and determined under her girlish powder and pinkness.*]

ROSALIE. Come with me.

JONATHAN. What?

ROSALIE. Leave and come with me.

JONATHAN [*Fearfully*]. Where?

ROSALIE. Anywhere.

JONATHAN. What . . . wha . . . what do you mean?

ROSALIE. I mean, let's leave. Let's run away. Far away. Tonight. Both of us, together. Let's run and run. Far, far away.

JONATHAN. You . . . mean, leave?

ROSALIE. Yes. *Leave.*

JONATHAN. Just like that?

ROSALIE. *Just like that.*

JONATHAN. But . . . but . . . but . . .

ROSALIE. You want to leave, don't you?

JONATHAN. I . . . I don't . . . don't know. I . . . I . . .

ROSALIE. What about the time you told me how much you'd like to go outside, how you'd love to walk by yourself, anywhere you wanted?

JONATHAN. I . . . I don't . . . know.

ROSALIE. Yes you do. Come. Give me your hand. Stop trembling so. Everything will be all right. Give me your hand and come with me. Just through the door. Then we're safe. Then we can run far away, somewhere where she'll never find us. Come, Jonathan. It's time to go. I've put on a new dress just for the occasion. I even had a key made so I could come and get you.

JONATHAN. There are others you could take.

ROSALIE. But I don't love them. [*Pause.*]

JONATHAN. You . . . you *love* me?

ROSALIE. Yes, Jonathan. I love you.

JONATHAN. Wha-wha-why?

ROSALIE [*Softly*]. Because you watch me every night.

JONATHAN. Well . . . can't we stay here?

ROSALIE. *No.*

JONATHAN. Wha-wha-whhhhy?

ROSALIE. Because I want you *alone.* [JONATHAN *turns from her and begins to walk about the room in confusion.*] I want you, Jonathan. Do you understand what I said? *I want you for my husband.*

JONATHAN. I . . . I . . . can't, I mean, I . . . I want to . . . go with you very much but I . . . I don't think . . . I can. I'm . . . sorry. [*He sits down and holds his head in his hands, sobbing quietly.*]

ROSALIE. What time will your mother be back?

JONATHAN. Na—not for a while.

ROSALIE. Are you sure?

JONATHAN. Ya-yes.

ROSALIE. Where is she?

JONATHAN. The usual place.

ROSALIE. What do you mean, "The usual place"?

JONATHAN [*With a sad laugh*]. The beach. [ROSALIE *looks at* JONATHAN *quizzically.*] She likes to look for people making love. Every night at midnight she walks down to the beach searching for people lying on blankets and making love. When she finds them she kicks sand in their faces and walks on. Sometimes it takes her as much as three hours to chase everyone away. [ROSALIE *smiles slightly and walks toward the master bedroom.* JONATHAN *freezes in fear. She puts her hand on the doorknob.*]

JONATHAN. WHAT ARE YOU DOING!? [*She smiles at him over her shoulder. She opens the door.*] STOP! You can't go in there! STOP! [*She opens the door completely and beckons to him.*]

ROSALIE. Come.

JONATHAN. Close it. Quickly!

ROSALIE. Come, Jonathan. Let's go inside.

JONATHAN. Close the door!

ROSALIE [*With a laugh*]. You've never been in here, have you?

JONATHAN. No. And you can't go in, either. No one can go in there but Mother. It's her room. Now close the door! [*She flicks on the light switch. No lights go on.*]

ROSALIE. What's wrong with the lights?

JONATHAN. There are none. . . . Mother's in mourning. [*Ros-ALIE walks into the room and pulls the drapes off the windows. Weird colored lights stream in and illuminate the bedroom in wild, distorted, nightmarish shadows and lights. They blink on and off, on and off. It's all like some strange, macabre fun house in an insane amusement park. Even the furniture in the room seems grotesque and distorted. The closet next to the bed seems peculiarly prominent. It almost seems to tilt over the bed.*]

JONATHAN [*Still in the main room*]. What have you done!? [ROSALIE *walks back to the door and smiles to him from within the master bedroom.*] What have you done?

ROSALIE. Come in, Jonathan.

JONATHAN. GET OUT OF THERE!

ROSALIE. Will you leave with me?

JONATHAN. I can't!

ROSALIE. But you want to, don't you?

JONATHAN. Yes, yes, I want to, but I told you . . . I . . . I . . . I can't. I can't! Do you understand? I can't! Now come out of there.

ROSALIE. Come in and get me.

JONATHAN Rosalie, *please.*

ROSALIE [*Bouncing on the bed*]. My, what a comfortable bed.

JONATHAN. [*Horrified*]. GET OFF THE BED!

ROSALIE. What soft, fluffy pillows. I think I'll take a nap.

JONATHAN. Rosalie, *please listen to me.* Come out of there. You're not supposed to be in that room. Please come out. Rosalie, *please.*

ROSALIE. Will you leave with me if I do?

JONATHAN. Rosalie . . . ? I'll . . . I'll show you my stamp collection if you'll promise to come out.

ROSALIE. Bring it in here.

JONATHAN. Will you come out then?

ROSALIE. Only if you bring it in here.

JONATHAN. But I'm not allowed to go in there.

ROSALIE [*Poutingly*]. Then I shan't come out!

JONATHAN. You've got to!

ROSALIE. Why?

JONATHAN. Mother will be back.

ROSALIE. She can sleep out there. [ROSALIE *yawns*.] I think I'll take a little nap. This bed is so comfortable. Really, Jonathan, you should come in and try it.

JONATHAN. MOTHER WILL BE BACK SOON!

ROSALIE. Give her your room, then, if you don't want her to sleep on the couch. I find it very nice in here. Good night. [*Pause*.]

JONATHAN. If I come in, will you come out?

ROSALIE. If you don't come in I'll never come out.

JONATHAN. And if I do?

ROSALIE. Then I may.

JONATHAN. What if I bring my stamps in?

ROSALIE. Bring them and find out. [*He goes to the dresser and takes out the drawer of stamps. Then he takes out the drawer of coins.*]

JONATHAN. I'm bringing the coins, too.

ROSALIE. How good you are, Jonathan. [*He takes a shelf full of books.*]

JONATHAN. My books, too. How's that? I'll show you my books

and my coins and my stamps. I'll show you them all. Then will you leave?

ROSALIE. Perhaps. [*He carries them all into the bedroom and sets them down next to the bed. He looks about fearfully.*]

ROSALIE. What's wrong?

JONATHAN. I've never been in here before.

ROSALIE. It's nothing but a room. There's nothing to be afraid of. [*He looks about doubtfully.*]

JONATHAN. Well, let me show you my stamps. I have one billion, five—

ROSALIE. Later, Jonathan. We'll have time. Let me show you something first.

JONATHAN. What's that?

ROSALIE. You're trembling.

JONATHAN. What do you want to show me?

ROSALIE. There's nothing to be nervous about. Come. Sit down.

JONATHAN. What do you want to show me?

ROSALIE. I can't show you if you won't sit down.

JONATHAN. I don't want to sit down! [*She takes hold of his hand. He pulls it away.*]

ROSALIE. Jonathan!

JONATHAN. You're sitting on Mother's bed.

ROSALIE. Then let's pretend it's my bed.

JONATHAN. It's not your bed!

ROSALIE. Come, Jonathan. Sit down here next to me.

JONATHAN. We've got to get out of here. Mother might come.

ROSALIE. Don't worry. We've got plenty of time. The beach is full of lovers.

JONATHAN. How do you know?

ROSALIE. I checked before I came. [Pause.]

JONATHAN. Let . . . let me show you my coins.

ROSALIE. Why are you trembling so?

JONATHAN. Look, we've got to get out! Something terrible will happen if we don't.

ROSALIE. Then leave with me.

JONATHAN. The bedroom?

ROSALIE. The hotel. The island. Your mother. Leave with me, Jonathan. Leave with me now, before it's too late.

JONATHAN. I . . . I . . . I . . .

ROSALIE. I love you, Jonathan, and I won't give you up. I want you . . . all for myself. Not to share with your mother, but for me, alone . . . to love, to live with, to have children by. I want you, Jonathan. You, whose skin is softer and whiter than any-one's I've ever known; whose voice is quiet and whose love is in every look of his eye. I want you, Jonathan, and I won't give you up. [Short pause.]

JONATHAN [*Softly, weakly*]. What do you want me to do?

ROSALIE. Forget about your mother. Pretend she never existed and look at me. Look at my eyes, Jonathan; my mouth, my hands, my skirt, my legs. Look at me, Jonathan. Are you still afraid?

JONATHAN. I'm not afraid. [*She smiles and starts to unbutton her dress.*] What are you doing!? No! [*She continues to unbutton her dress.*]

ROSALIE. Your mother is strong, but I am stronger. [*She rises and her skirt falls about her feet. She stands in a slip and crinolines.*] I don't look so pink and girlish any more, do I? [*She laughs.*] But you want me anyhow. You're ashamed but you want me anyhow. It's written on your face. And I'm very glad. Because I want you. [*She takes off a crinoline.*]

JONATHAN. PUT IT ON! *Please,* put it back on!

ROSALIE. Come, Jonathan. [*She takes off another crinoline.*] Lie down. Let me loosen your shirt.

JONATHAN. No . . . NO . . . NO! STOP! *Please,* stop! [*She takes her last crinoline off and reaches down to take off her socks. The lights outside blink weirdly. Wild, jagged music with a drum beating in the background is heard.*]

ROSALIE. Don't be afraid, Jonathan. Come. Lie down. Everything will be wonderful. [*She takes her socks off and lies down in her slip. She drops a strap over one shoulder and smiles.*]

JONATHAN. Get off my mother's bed!

ROSALIE. I want you, Jonathan, all for my own. Come. The bed is soft. Lie here by my side.

She reaches up and takes his hand. Meekly he sits down on the edge of the bed. The closet door swings open suddenly and the corpse of Albert Edward Robinson Rosepettle III tumbles forward stiffly and onto the bed, his stone-stiff arms falling across Rosalie's *legs, his head against her side.* Jonathan, *too terrified to scream, puts his hand across his mouth and sinks down onto the bed, almost in a state of collapse. Outside the music screams.*

Rosalie. Who the hell is this!?

Jonathan. It-it-it-it . . . it . . . it's . . .

Rosalie. What a stupid place to keep a corpse. [*She pushes him back in the closet and shuts the door.*] Forget it, Jonathan. I put him back in the closet. Everything's fine again.

Jonathan. It's . . . it's . . . it's my . . . my . . . my . . .

Rosalie [*Kneeling next to him on the bed and starting to unbutton his shirt.*] It's all right, Jonathan. It's all right. Sshh. Come. Let me take off your clothes.

Jonathan [*Still staring dumbly into space*]. It's . . . it's my . . . ffffather.

The closet door swings open again and the corpse falls out, this time his arms falling about Rosalie's *neck.* Jonathan *almost swoons.*

Rosalie. Oh, for God's sake. [*She pushes the corpse off the bed and onto the floor.*] Jonathan . . . ? LISTEN TO ME, JONATHAN! STOP LOOKING AT HIM AND LOOK AT ME! [*He looks away from his father, fearfully, his mouth open in terror.*] I love you, Jonathan, and I want you *now.* Not later and not as partner with your mother but now and by myself. I want you, Jonathan, as my husband. I want you to lie with me, to sleep with me, to be with me, to kiss me and touch me, to live with me, *forever.* Stop looking at him! He's dead! Listen to me. I'm alive. I want you for my husband! Now help me take my slip

off Then you can look at my body and touch me. Come, Jonathan.
Lie down. I want you forever.

JONATHAN. Ma-Mother was right! You *do* let men do anything
they want to you.

ROSALIE. Of course she was right! Did you really think I was
that sweet and pure? Everything she said was right. [*She laughs.*]
Behind the bushes and it's done. One-two-three and it's done.
Here's the money. Thanks. Come again. Hah-hah! Come again!
[*Short pause.*] So what!? It's only you I love. They make no dif-
ference.

JONATHAN. You're dirty! [*He tries to get up but can't, for his
father is lying in front of his feet.*]

ROSALIE. No, I'm not dirty. I'm full of love and womanly feelings. I want children. Tons of them. I want a husband. Is that
dirty?

JONATHAN. You're dirty!

ROSALIE. No. I'm pure. I want no one but you. I renounce
all past lovers. They were mistakes. I confess my indiscretions.
Now you know all so I'm pure again. Take off your clothes.

JONATHAN. NO!

ROSALIE. Forget about your father. Drop your pants on top of
him, then you won't see his face. Forget about your mother. She's
gone. Forget them both and look at me. Love is so beautiful,
Jonathan. Come and let me love you; tonight and forever. Come
and let me keep you mine. Mine to love when I want, mine to
kiss when I want, mine to have when I want. Mine. All mine.
So come, Jonathan. Come and close your eyes. It's better that
way. Close your eyes so you can't see. Close your eyes and let
me lie with you. Let me show you how beautiful it is . . . love.

[*She lies back in bed and slowly starts to raise her slip.* JONATHAN
*stares at her legs in horror. Then, suddenly, he seizes her crumpled
skirt and throws it over her face. He smothers her to death.* . . .
*At last he rises and, picking up his box of stamps, dumps the
stamps over her limp body. He does the same with his coins and
finally his books, until at last she is buried. Then, done, he throws
his hands over his eyes and turns to run. But as he staggers past
the corpse of his father, his father's lifeless arms somehow come
to life for an instant and, reaching out, grab Jonathan by the feet.*
JONATHAN *falls to the floor. For a moment he lies there, stretched
across his father's body, too terrified to move. But a soft, ethereal-
green light begins to suffuse the room and heavenly harp music
is heard in the air. As if his body had suddenly become immortal
and weightless,* JONATHAN *rises up from the floor and with long,
slow, dreamlike steps* (*like someone walking under water*), *he
floats through the bedroom door and drifts across the living
room, picking up his telescope on the way. He floats out to the
balcony and begins to scan the sky. The harp music grows louder
and more paradisiacal: Debussy in Heaven. While under the harp
music, soft, muffled laughter can be heard; within the bedroom,
within the living room, from the rear of the theater, laughter all
about.*]
His mother tiptoes into the living room. Her air is awry, her
hat is on crooked, her blouse hangs wrinkled and out of her
pants. Her legs are covered with sand.

MADAME ROSEPETTLE. Twenty-three couples. I annoyed twenty-
three couples, all of them coupled in various positions, all equally
distasteful. It's a record, that's what it is. It's a record! [*Breathing
heavily from excitement she begins to tuck in her blouse and
straighten her hair. She notices the chaotic state of the room. She
shrieks slightly.*] What has happened!? [*She notices the* PLANTS.]
My plants! [*She notices the* FISH.] Rosalinda! Great gods, my
fish has lost her water! ALBERT! ALBERT! [*She searches about
the room for her* SON. *She sees him standing on the porch.*] Ah,
there you are. Edward, what has been going on during my brief
absence? What are you doing out here when Rosalinda is lying

in there dead? DEAD!? Oh God, dead. Robinson, answer me.
What are you looking for? I've told you there's nothing out there.
This place is a madhouse. That's what it is. A madhouse. [*She
turns and walks into her bedroom. An airplane is heard flying
in the distance. JONATHAN scans the horizon frantically. The plane
grows nearer. Jonathan follows it with his telescope. It flies
overhead. It begins to circle about. Wildly, desperately, Jonathan
waves his arms to the plane. . . . It flies away.*]

MADAME ROSEPETTLE *re-enters the room.*

Robinson! I went to lie down and I stepped on your father!
I lay down and I lay on some girl. Robinson, there is a woman on
my bed and I do believe she's stopped breathing. What is more,
you've buried her under your fabulous collection of stamps, coins,
and books. I ask you, Robinson. As a mother to a son I ask you.
What is the meaning of this?

Blackout and Curtain.

INDIANS

For Leslie

ACKNOWLEDGMENTS

The idea for this play occurred to me in March 1966. Since then, there have been many persons whose help has been instrumental in the play's reaching its final form: first, my producer, Lyn Austin, to whom I described its basic concept, and who gave me an advance of money so I could afford to research the necessary historical material; then, the wonderful actors and staff of the Royal Shakespeare Company, who presented the play some two years later, and especially Jack Gelber, who directed the excellent London production, and whose firsthand knowledge of the American Indians was constantly invaluable; Zelda Fitchandler and the staff and actors of the Arena Stage, where the next and greatly rewritten version of the play was produced, which afforded me still another relatively unstressful opportunity to view what I had written; Gene Frankel, who staged the Washington and New York productions and asked a seemingly endless number of incisive, important, and fundamental questions; my late agent, Audrey Wood, who—with great affection—kept urging further rewrites, and who only smiled when I said I thought this enterprise threatened to become a lifelong task. I would particularly like to thank the Rockefeller Foundation, which gave me a grant of money so my wife and I could live in Europe during the time my play was in production there, and then allowed us to go, immediately after the production, to the fantastic Villa Serbelloni, at Lake Como, where the basic rethinking and fundamental reshaping of the play was done.

Indians was first performed by the Royal Shakespeare Company on July 4, 1968, at the Aldwych Theatre, London. Its American premiere was on May 6, 1969, at the Arena Stage, Washington, D.C.

Characters

Indians opened in New York at the Brooks Atkinson Theatre on October 13, 1969, with the following cast:

BUFFALO BILL   Stacy Keach
SITTING BULL   Manu Tupou
SENATOR LOGAN   Tom Aldredge
SENATOR DAWES   Richard McKenzie
SENATOR MORGAN   Jon Richards
TRIAL SOLDIERS   Bob Hamilton, Richard Nieves
JOHN GRASS   Sam Waterston
SPOTTED TAIL   James J. Sloyan
GRAND DUKE ALEXIS   Raul Julia
INTERPRETER   Yusef Bulos
NED BUNTLINE   Charles Durning
GERONIMO   Ed Rombola
MASTER VALET   Darryl Croxton
FIRST LADY   Dortha Duckworth
OL' TIME PRESIDENT   Peter MacLean
WILD BILL HICKOK   Barton Heyman
TESKANJAVILA   Dimitra Arliss
UNCAS   Raul Julia
WHITE HOUSE ORCHESTRA   Tony Posk, Peter Rosenfelt
VALETS   Joseph Ragno, Richard Novello, Brian Donohue
CHIEF JOSEPH   George Mitchell

ANNIE OAKLEY Pamela Grey
JESSE JAMES Ronny Cox
BILLY THE KID Ed Rombola
PONCHO Raul Julia
BARTENDER Brian Donohue
COWBOYS Richard Nieves, Richard Miller, Clint Allmon, Bob
  Hamilton
COLONEL FORSYTH Peter MacLean
LIEUTENANT Richard Novello
REPORTERS Ronny Cox, Brian Donohue, Darryl Croxton
CRAZY HORSE Dino Laudicina
HE-WHO-HEARS-THUNDER Robert McLean
RED CLOUD Andy Torres
LITTLE HAWK Jay Fletcher
KIOKUK Princeton Dean
SATANTA Ed Henkel
OLD TAZA Michael Ebbin
BLACK HAWK Kevin Conway
TECUMSEH Pascual Vaquer
YELLOW CLOUD Wesley Fata
KICKING BEAR Gary Weber
TOUCH-THE-CLOUDS Peter DeMaio
HOWLING WOLF Ted Goodridge
WHITE ANTELOPE Tom Fletcher
LOW DOG Philip Arsenault
NAICHE Juan Antonio
INDIAN DRUMMERS Leon Oxman, Allan Silverman

Director, Gene Frankel; Setting, Oliver Smith; Lighting, Thomas
Skelton; Costumes, Marjorie Slaiman; Music, Richard Peaslee;
Choreography, Julie Arenal; Associate Producer, Steven Sinn;
Production Assistant, Binti Hoskins

Chronology for a Dreamer

1846   William F. Cody born in Le Claire, Iowa, on February 26.

1866   Geronimo surrenders.

1868   William Cody accepts employment to provide food for railroad workers; kills 4,280 buffaloes. Receives nickname "Buffalo Bill."

1869   *Buffalo Bill, the King of the Border Men,* a dime novel by Ned Buntline, makes Buffalo Bill a national hero.

1872   Expedition west in honor of Grand Duke Alexis of Russia, Buffalo Bill as guide.

1876   Battle at the Little Big Horn; Custer killed.

1877   Chief Joseph surrenders.

1878   Buffalo Bill plays himself in *Scouts of the Plains,* a play by Ned Buntline.

1879   Wild Bill Hickok joins Buffalo Bill on the stage.

1883   Sitting Bull surrenders, is sent to Standing Rock Reservation.

1883   "Buffalo Bill's Wild West Show" gives first performance, is great success.

1885   Sitting Bull allowed to join Wild West Show, tours with company for a year.

1886 United States Commission visits Standing Rock Reservation to investigate Indian grievances.

1890 Sitting Bull assassinated, December 15.

1890 Wounded Knee Massacre, December 25.

The play derives, in part, from this chronology but does not strictly adhere to it.—A.K.

Scene 1

(*Audience enters to stage with no curtain. House lights dim. On stage: three large glass cases, one holding a larger-than-life-size effigy of Buffalo Bill in fancy embroidered buckskin. One, an effigy of Sitting Bull dressed in simple buckskin or cloth, no headdress, little if any ornamentation. The last case contains some artifacts: a buffalo skull, a bloodstained Indian shirt, and an old rifle. The surrounding stage is dark. The cases are lit by spotlights from above.*

Strange music coming from all about. Sense of dislocation.

The house lights fade to dark.

Music up.

Lights on the cases slowly dim.

Sound of wind, soft at first.

The cases glide into the shadowy distance and disappear.

Eerie light now on stage; dim spotlights sweep the floor as if trying to locate something in space.

Brief, distorted strains of Western American music.

A VOICE *reverberates from all about the theatre.*

VOICE

Cody . . . Cody . . . Cody! . . . CODY!

(*One of the spotlights passes something: a man on a horse. The spotlight slowly retraces itself, picks up the horse and rider. They are in a far corner of the stage; they move in slow motion.*

The other spotlights now move toward them, until all converge. At first, the light is dim. As they come toward us, it gets brighter.

The man is BUFFALO BILL, *dressed as in the museum case. The horse is a glorious white artificial stallion with wild, glowing eyes.*

They approach slowly, their slow motion gradually becoming normal speed.

Vague sound of cheering heard. Music becoming rodeolike. More identifiable.

Then, slowly, from the floor, an open-framed oval fence rises and encloses them.

The horse shies.

Tiny lights, strung beneath the top bar of the fence, glitter faintly. The spotlights—multicolored—begin to crisscross about the oval.

Ghostly-pale Wild West Show banners slowly descend.

Then! It's a WILD WEST SHOW!

Loud, brassy music!

Lights blazing everywhere!

The horse rears. His rider whispers a few words, calms him.

Then, a great smile on his face, BUFFALO BILL *begins to tour the ring, one hand lightly gripping the reins, the other proudly waving his big Stetson to the unseen surrounding crowd. Surely it is a great sight; the horse prances, struts, canters, dances to the music, leaps softly through the light,* BUFFALO BILL *effortlessly in control of the whole world, the universe; eternity.)*

   BUFFALO BILL

Yessir, BACK AGAIN! That triumphant brassy music, those familiar savage drums! Should o' known I couldn't stay away! Should o' known here's where I belong! The heat o' that ol' spotlight on my face. Yessir. . . . Should o' known here's where I belong. . . .

(*He takes a deep breath, closes his eyes, savors the air. A pause.*)

Reminded o' somethin' tol' me once by General Custer. You remember him—one o' the great dumbass men in history. Not fer nothin' that he graduated last in his class at West Point! Anyways, we was out on the plains one day, when he turned t' me, with a kind o' far-off look in his eye, an' said, "Bill! If there is one thing a man must never fear, it's makin' a personal comeback."

(*He chuckles.*)

Naturally, I——

VOICE

(*Softly.*)

And now, to start . . .

BUFFALO BILL

(*Startled.*)

Hm?

VOICE

And now to start.

BUFFALO BILL

But I . . . just . . . got up here.

VOICE

I'm sorry; it's time to start.

BUFFALO BILL

Can't you *wait a second?* WHAT'S THE RUSH? *WAIT A SECOND!*

(*Silence. He takes a deep breath; quiets his horse down.*)

I'm sorry. But if I seem a trifle edgy to you, it's only 'cause I've just come from a truly harrowing engagement; seems my . . . manager, a . . . rather *ancient* gentleman, made a terrible *mistake* an' booked me int' what turned out t' be a ghost town! Well! I dunno what you folks know 'bout show business, but le' me tell you, there is nothin' more depressin' than playin' two-a-day in a goddam ghost town!

(*He chuckles.*

INDIANS *appear around the outside of the ring.*
The horse senses their presence and shies; BUFFALO BILL, *as if realizing what it means, turns in terror.*)
>   VOICE
> Bill.
>   BUFFALO BILL
> But——
>   VOICE
> It's *time.*
> (*Pause.*)
>   BUFFALO BILL
> Be—before we start, I'd . . . just like to say——
>   VOICE
> Bill!
> (*The* INDIANS *slowly approach.*)
>   BUFFALO BILL
> ——*to say* that . . . I am a fine man. And anyone who says otherwise is *WRONG!*
>   VOICE
> (*Softly.*)
> Bill, *it's time.*
>   BUFFALO BILL
> My life is an open book; I'm not *ashamed* of its bein' looked at!
>   VOICE
> (*Coaxing tone.*)
> *Bill* . . .
>   BUFFALO BILL
> I'm sorry, this is very . . . hard . . . for me t' say. But I believe I . . . am a . . . hero. . . . *A GODDAM HERO!*
> (*Indian music.*
> *His horse rears wildly.*
> *Lights change for next scene.*)

Scene 2

(*Light up on* SITTING BULL. *He is dressed simply—no feathered headdress. It is winter.*)

SITTING BULL

I am Sitting Bull! . . . In the moon of the first snow-falling, in the year half my people died from hunger, the Great Father sent three wise men . . . to investigate the conditions of our reservation, though we'd been promised he would come himself.

(*Lights up on* SENATORS LOGAN, MORGAN, *and* DAWES; *they are flanked by armed* SOLDIERS. *Opposite them, in a semicircle, are* SITTING BULL's *people, all huddling in tattered blankets from the cold.*)

SENATOR LOGAN

Indians! Please be assured that this committee has not come to punish you or take away any of your land but only to hear your grievances, determine if they are just. And if so, remedy them. For we, like the Great Father, wish only the best for our Indian children.

(*The* SENATORS *spread out various legal documents.*)

SITTING BULL

They were accompanied by . . . my friend, William Cody——
(*Enter* BUFFALO BILL, *collar of his overcoat turned up for the wind.*)

in whose Wild West Show I'd once appeared . . .

(BUFFALO BILL *greets a number of the* INDIANS.)

in exchange for some food, a little clothing. And a beautiful
horse that could do tricks.

SENATOR MORGAN
Colonel Cody has asked if he might say a few words before
testimony begins.

SENATOR LOGAN
We would be honored.

BUFFALO BILL
(*To the* INDIANS.)
My . . . brothers.
(*Pause.*)
I know how disappointed you all must be that the Great Father
isn't here; I apologize for having said I thought I . . . could
bring him.
(*Pause.*)
However! The three men I *have* brought are by far his most
trusted personal representatives. And I promise that talking to
them will be the same as . . .
(*Pause. Softly.*)
. . . talking to him.
(*Long pause; he rubs his eyes as if to soothe a headache.*)
To . . . Sitting Bull, then . . .
(*He stares at* SITTING BULL.)
. . . I would like to say that I hope you can overlook your . . .
disappointment. And remember what is at *stake* here. And not
get angry . . . or too impatient.
(*Pause.*)
Also, I hope you will ask your people to speak with open hearts
when talking to these men. And treat them with the same great
respect I have always . . . shown . . . to you, for these men
have come to *help* you and your people. And I am afraid they
may be the only ones left, now, who can.

SITTING BULL
And though there were many among us who wanted to speak
first: men like Red Cloud! And Little Hawk! And He-Who-
Hears-Thunder! And Crazy Horse! Men who were great war-

riors, and had counted many coups! And been with us at the
Little Big Horn when we *KILLED CUSTER!* . . .
(*Pause.*)
I would not let them speak. . . . For they were like me, and
tended to get angry, easily.
(*Pause.*)
Instead, I asked the *young* man, John Grass, who had never
fought at all, but had been to the white man's school at Carlisle.
And *thought* he understood . . . something . . . of their ways.
 BUFFALO BILL
Sitting Bull would like John Grass to speak first.
 LOGAN
Call John Grass.
 BUFFALO BILL
John Grass! Come forward.
(*Enter* JOHN GRASS *in a black cutaway many sizes too small for
him. He wears an Indian shirt. Around his neck is a medal.*)
 JOHN GRASS
Brothers! I am going to talk about what the Great Father told
us a long time ago. He told us to give up hunting and start
farming. So we did as he said, and our people grew hungry. For
the land was suited to grazing not farming, and even if we'd
been farmers, nothing could have grown. So the Great Father
said he would send us food and clothing, but nothing came of
it. So we asked him for the money he had promised us when
we sold him the Black Hills, thinking, with this money we
could *buy* food and clothing. But nothing came of it. So we
grew ill and sad. . . . So to help us from this sadness, he sent
Bishop Marty, to teach us to be Christians. But when we told
him we did not wish to be Christians but wished to be like our
fathers, and dance the sundance, and fight bravely against
the Shawnee and the Crow! And pray to the Great Spirits who
made the four winds, and the earth, and made man from the
dust of this earth, Bishop Marty hit us! . . . So we said to the
Great Father that we thought we would like to go *back* to
hunting, because to live, we needed food. But we found that

while we had been learning to farm, the buffalo had gone away. And the plains were filled now only with their bones. . . . Before we give you any more of our land, or move from here where the people we loved are growing white in their coffins, we want you to tell the Great Father to give us, who still live, what he promised he would! *No more than that.*

SITTING BULL

I prayed for the return of the buffalo!

(*Lights fade to black on everyone but* BUFFALO BILL.

Distant gunshot heard offstage.

Pause.

Two more gunshots.

Lights to black on BUFFALO BILL.)

Scene 3

(*Light up on* SPOTTED TAIL, *standing on a ledge above the plains.*
It is night, and he is lit by a pale moon.
The air is hot. No wind.
A rifle shot is heard offstage, of much greater presence than the previous shots.
SPOTTED TAIL *peers in its direction.*
Sound, offstage, of wounded bulls.
Enter an INDIAN *dressed as a buffalo, wounded in the eye and bellowing with pain.*
He circles the stage.
Enter two more buffaloes, also wounded in the eyes.
The first buffalo dies.
The two other buffaloes stagger over to his side and die beside him; another buffalo [missing an eye] enters, staggers in a circle, senses the location of the dead buffaloes and heads dizzily toward them—dying en route, halfway there.
SPOTTED TAIL *crouches and gazes down at them. Then he stares up at the sky.*
Night creatures screech in the dark.
A pause.)
    BUFFALO BILL

(*Offstage but coming closer.*)

Ninety-three, ninety-four, ninety-five . . . ninety-*six! I DID IT!*

(*Enter, running, a much younger* BUFFALO BILL, *rifle in hand, followed shortly by* MEMBERS OF THE U. S. CAVALRY *bearing torches, and the* GRAND DUKE'S INTERPRETER.)

I did it, I did it! No one believed I could, but *I did it!* One hundred buffalo—one hundred shots! "You jus' gimme some torches," I said. "I *know* there's buffalo around us. *Here.* Put yer ear t' the ground. Feel it tremblin'? Well. You wanna see somethin' fantastic, you get me some torches. I'll shoot the reflections in their eyes. I'll shoot 'em like they was so many shiny nickels!"

INTERPRETER

I'll tell the Grand Duke you did what you said. I know he'll be pleased.

BUFFALO BILL

Well he oughta be! I don' give exhibitions like this fer just anybody!

(*Exit the* INTERPRETER.)

'Specially as these critters're gettin' so damn hard t' find.

(*To the* SOLDIERS.)

Not like the ol' days when I was huntin' 'em fer the railroads. (*He laughs, gazes down at one of the buffaloes. Pause. He looks away; squints as if in pain.*)

A SOLDIER

Are you all right, sir?

BUFFALO BILL

Uh . . . yes. Fine.

(*Exit the* SOLDIERS.

BUFFALO BILL *rubs his head.*

SPOTTED TAIL *hops down from his perch and walks up behind* CODY *unnoticed; stares at him.*

Pause.

BUFFALO BILL *senses the Indian's presence and turns, cocking his rifle. The Indian makes no move.*

BUFFALO BILL *stares at the Indian.*

Pause.)

BUFFALO BILL

Spotted Tail! My God. I haven't seen you in years. How . . . ya been?

(*Slight laugh.*)

SPOTTED TAIL

What are you doing here?

(*Pause.*)

BUFFALO BILL

Well, well, what . . . are *you* doing here? This isn't Sioux territory!

SPOTTED TAIL

It isn't *your* territory either.

(*Pause.*)

BUFFALO BILL

Well I'm with . . . these *people.* I'm scoutin' for 'em.

SPOTTED TAIL

These people . . . must be very hungry.

BUFFALO BILL

Hm?

SPOTTED TAIL

To need so many buffalo.

BUFFALO BILL

Ah! Of course! You were following the buffalo *also!* . . . Well listen, I'm sure my friends won't mind you takin' some. 'Tween us, my friends don't 'specially care for the *taste* o' buffalo meat.

(*He laughs.*)

My God, but it's good t' see you again!

SPOTTED TAIL

Your friends: I have been studying them from the hills. They are very strange. They seem neither men, nor women.

BUFFALO BILL
Well! Actually, they're sort of a new *breed* o' people. Called dudes.
(*He chuckles.*)
SPOTTED TAIL
You *like* them?
BUFFALO BILL
Well . . . sure. Why not?
(*Pause.*)
I mean, obviously, they ain't the sort I've been used to. But then, things're changin' out here. An' these men are the ones who're changin' 'em. So, if you wanna be *part* o' these things, an' not left behind somewhere, you jus' plain hafta get *used* to 'em. You—uh—follow . . . what I mean?
(*Silence.*)
I mean . . . you've got to *adjust.* To the times. Make a *plan* fer yerself. I have one. You should have one, too. Fer yer own good. Believe me.
(*Long pause.*)
SPOTTED TAIL
What is your plan?
BUFFALO BILL
Well, my plan is t' help people. Like you, ferinstance. Or these people I'm with. More . . . even . . . than that, maybe. And, and, whatever . . . it is I *do* t' help, for it, these people may someday jus' possibly name streets after me. Cities. Counties. States! I'll . . . be as famous as Dan'l Boone! . . . An' somewhere, on top of a beautiful mountain that overlooks more plains 'n rivers than any other mountain, there might even be a statue of me sittin' on a great white horse, a-wavin' my hat t' everyone down below, thankin' 'em, fer thankin' me, fer havin' done . . . whatever . . . it is I'm gonna . . . *do* fer 'em all. How . . . come you got such a weird look on yer face?
BUNTLINE
(*Offstage.*)
HEY, CODY! *STAY WHERE YA ARE!*

BUFFALO BILL
DON' WORRY! I AIN'T BUDGIN'!
(*To* SPOTTED TAIL.)
That's Mister Ned Buntline, the well-known newspaper re-
porter. I think he's gonna do an *article* on me! General Custer,
who's in charge, an' I think is pushin' fer an article on *himself*,
says this may well be the most important western expedition
since Lewis 'n Clark.
BUNTLINE
(*Offstage.*)
BY THE WAY, *WHERE* ARE YA?
BUFFALO BILL
I . . . AIN'T SURE! JUST HEAD FOR THE LIGHTS!
(*He laughs to himself.*)
SPOTTED TAIL
Tell me. Who is the man everyone always bows to?
BUFFALO BILL
Oh! The Gran' Duke! He's from a place called Russia. This
whole shindig's in his honor. I'm sure he'd love t' meet you.
He's never seen a real Indian.
SPOTTED TAIL
There are no Indians in Russia?
(BUFFALO BILL *shakes his head.*)
Then I will study him even more carefully than the others.
Maybe if he takes me back to Russia with him, I will not end
like my people will . . . end.
BUFFALO BILL
(*Startled.*)
What?
SPOTTED TAIL
I mean, like these fools here, on the ground.
(*He stares at the buffalo.*)
BUFFALO BILL
Ah . . . Well, if ya don' mind my sayin', I think you're bein'
a bit pessimistic. But you do what ya like. Jus' remember: these
people you're studyin'—some folk think *they're* the fools.

SPOTTED TAIL

Oh, no! They are not fools! *No one who is a white man can be a fool.*
(*He smiles coldly at Buffalo Bill; heraldic Russian fanfare off-stage.*

Enter RUSSIAN TORCHBEARERS *and* TRUMPETEERS.

BUFFALO BILL *and* SPOTTED TAIL, *in awe, back away.*

Enter with much pomp and ceremony GRAND DUKE ALEXIS *on a splendid litter carved like a horse. He is accompanied by his* INTERPRETER, *who points out the four buffaloes to the* GRAND DUKE *as he majestically circles the clearing. He is followed by* NED BUNTLINE, *who carries a camera and tripod.*)

BUFFALO BILL

My God, but that is a beautiful sight!
(*The* GRAND DUKE *comes to a halt. Majestic sweep of his arms to those around him.*)

GRAND DUKE

(*Makes a regal Russian speech.*)

INTERPRETER

His Excellency the Grand Duke wishes to express his heart-felt admiration of Buffalo Bill . . .
(*Music up.*)
. . . for having done what he has done tonight.
(*The* GRAND DUKE *gestures majestically. The* INTERPRETER *opens a small velvet box. Airy music. The* INTERPRETER *walks toward* BUFFALO BILL.)

GRAND DUKE

(*Gesturing for* BUFFALO BILL *to come forward.*)
Boofilo Beel!
(BUFFALO BILL *walks solemnly forward. The* INTERPRETER *takes out a medal.* BUFFALO BILL, *deeply moved, looks around, embarrassed.*

The INTERPRETER *smiles and holds up the medal, gestures warmly for* BUFFALO BILL *to kneel. He does so.*

The INTERPRETER *places the medal, which is on a bright ribbon, around his neck.*

Flashgun goes off.)

BUNTLINE

Great picture, Cody! FRONT PAGE! My God, what a night!
What a story! Uh . . . sorry, yer Highness. Didn't mean t'
distoib ya.
(*He backs meekly away. Sets up his camera for another shot.
The* GRAND DUKE *regains his composure.*)

GRAND DUKE

(*Russian speech.*)

INTERPRETER

His Excellency wonders how Buffalo Bill became such a deadly
shot.

BUFFALO BILL

Oh, well, you know, just . . . practice.
(*Embarrassed laugh.*)

GRAND DUKE

(*Russian speech.*)

INTERPRETER

His Excellency says he wishes that his stupid army knew how
to practice.

GRAND DUKE

(*Russian speech.*)

INTERPRETER

Better yet, he wishes you would come back with him to his
palace and protect him yourself.

BUFFALO BILL

Oh.
(*Slight laugh.*)
Well, I'm sure the Grand Duke's in excellent hands.
(*The* INTERPRETER *whispers what* BUFFALO BILL *has just said.*)

GRAND DUKE

Da! *Hands.*
(*He holds out his hands, then turns them and puts them around
his throat.*)

BUFFALO BILL

I think His Majesty's exaggeratin'. I can't believe he's not *sur-
rounded* by friends.

GRAND DUKE

FRIENDS!

(*He cackles and draws his sword, slashes the air.*)

Friends! Friends! . . . *Friends!*

(*He fights them off.*)

BUFFALO BILL

(*To* BUNTLINE.)

I think he's worried 'bout somethin'.

BUNTLINE

Very strange behavior.

GRAND DUKE

(*Nervous Russian speech.*)

INTERPRETER

His Excellency wonders if Buffalo Bill has ever been afraid.

BUFFALO BILL

. . . Afraid?

GRAND DUKE

(*Russian word.*)

INTERPRETER

Outnumbered.

BUFFALO BILL

Ah.

(*Slight laugh.*)

Well, uh——

BUNTLINE

Go on, tell 'm. It'll help what I'm plannin' t' write.

BUFFALO BILL

(*Delighted.*)

It *will?*

BUNTLINE

Absolutely. Look: de West is changin'—right? Well, people wanna know about it. Wanna feel . . . *part* o' things. I think *you're* what dey need. Someone t' listen to, observe, *identify* wid. No, no, really! I been studyin' you.

BUFFALO BILL

. . . You have?

BUNTLINE

I think you could be de inspiration o' dis land.

BUFFALO BILL

Now I *know* you're foolin'!

BUNTLINE

Not at all. . . . Well go on. Tell 'm what he wants t' hear. T'rough my magic pen, others will hear also. . . . Donmentionit. De nation needs men like me, too.

(*He pats* CODY *on the shoulder and shoves him off toward the* GRAND DUKE; CODY *gathers his courage.*)

BUFFALO BILL

(*To the* GRAND DUKE.)

Well, uh . . . where can I begin? Certainly it's true that I've been outnumbered. And—uh—many times. Yes.

BUNTLINE

That's the way.

BUFFALO BILL

More times, in fact, than I can count.

BUNTLINE

Terrific.

BUFFALO BILL

(*Warming to the occasion.*)

An' believe me, I can count pretty high!

BUNTLINE

SENSATIONAL!

BUFFALO BILL

Mind you, 'gainst *me*, twelve's normally an even battle—long's I got my two six-shooters that is.

BUNTLINE

Keep it up, keep it up!

BUFFALO BILL

THIRTEEN! If one of 'em's thin enough for a bullet t' go clean through. Fourteen if I got a huntin' knife. Fifteen if there's a hard surface off o' which I can ricochet a few shots.

BUNTLINE

Go on!

BUFFALO BILL

Um, twenty . . . if I got a stick o' dynamite. HUNDRED! IF THERE'S ROCKS T' START A AVALANCHE!

(BUNTLINE *applauds.*)

What I mean is, with *me* it's never say die! Why . . . I remember once I was ridin' for the Pony Express 'tween Laramie 'n Tombstone. Suddenly, jus' past the Pecos, fifty drunk Comanches attack. Noise like a barroom whoop-di-do, arrows fallin' like hailstones! I mean, they come on me so fast they don' have time t' see my face, notice who I am, realize I'm in fact a very good *friend* o' theirs!

GRAND DUKE

FRIEND! FRIEND!

BUNTLINE

(*Sotto voce.*)

Get off de subject!

BUFFALO BILL

Well, there was no alternative but t' fire back. Well I'd knocked off 'bout thirty o' their number when I realized I was *out* o' bullets. Just at that moment, a arrow whizzed past my head. Thinkin' fast, I reached out an' caught it. Then, usin' it like a fly swatter, I knocked away the other nineteen arrows that were headin' fer my heart. Whereupon, I stood up in the stirrups, hurled the arrow sixty yards. . . . An' killed their chief.

(*Pause.*)

Which . . . *depressed* . . . the remainin' Indians.

(*Pause.*)

And sent 'em scurryin' home. Well! That's sort o' what ya might call a typical day!

(*Bravos from everyone except the* GRAND DUKE.)

GRAND DUKE

(*Russian speech, quite angry.*)

INTERPRETER

His Excellency says he would like to kill a Comanche also.

BUFFALO BILL
Hm?

GRAND DUKE
(*With obvious jealousy.*)
Like Boofilo Beel!

INTERPRETER
Like Buffalo Bill!

GRAND DUKE
(*Excited Russian speech.*)

INTERPRETER
He will *prove* he cannot be intimidated!

GRAND DUKE
Rifle, rifle, rifle!

BUFFALO BILL
(*To* BUNTLINE.)
I think my story may've worked a bit too well.

BUNTLINE
Nonsense! This is *terrific!*
(*They duck as the* GRAND DUKE, *cackling madly, scans the surrounding darkness over his rifle sight.*)
Shows you've won the Grand Duke's heart.

GRAND DUKE
(*Pounding his chest.*)
Boofilo Beel! *I* . . . am *BOOFILO BEEL!*
(*He laughs demonically.*)

BUNTLINE
I think you'd better find 'm a Comanche.

BUFFALO BILL
Right! *Well.* Um . . .
(*Slight laugh.*)
That *could* be a . . . problem.

GRAND DUKE
Comanche! *Comanche!*

BUFFALO BILL
Ya see, fer one thing, the Comanches live in Texas. And we're
in Missouri.

GRAND DUKE
COMANCHE! *COMANCHE!*

BUFFALO BILL
Fer another, I ain't 'xactly sure what they look like.

GRAND DUKE
Ah!
(*He fires into the darkness.*

SPOTTED TAIL *stumbles out, collapses and dies.*

The GRAND DUKE *and his* INTERPRETER *delirious with joy.* BUNT-LINE *dumfounded.* BUFFALO BILL *stunned, but for vastly different reasons.*)

BUNTLINE
(*Approaching the body cautiously.*)
My God, will you look at that? Fate must be smiling!
(*He laughs weakly, stares up at the heavens in awe.*

BUFFALO BILL, *almost in a trance, walks over to the body; stares down at it.*

Weird music heard.

The lights change color, grow vague.

All movement arrested.

SPOTTED TAIL *rises slowly and moves just as slowly toward the* GRAND DUKE; *stops.*)

SPOTTED TAIL
My name is Spotted Tail. My father was a Sioux; my mother, part Cherokee, part Crow. No matter how you look at it, I'm just not a Comanche.
(*He sinks back to the ground.*

Lights return to normal, the music ends.)

GRAND DUKE
(*Baffled Russian speech.*)

INTERPRETER
His Excellency would like to know what the man he just shot has said.
(*Long pause.* BUFFALO BILL *looks around, as if for help; all eyes upon him.*)

BUFFALO BILL
(*Softly.*)
He said . . .
(*Pause.*)
"I . . .
(*Pause.*)
should have . . .
(*He looks at* BUNTLINE, *takes a deep breath.*)
stayed at home in . . . Texas with the rest of my . . . Comanche tribe."
BUNTLINE
Fabulous!
(*He takes* SPOTTED TAIL's *picture; the night sky glows from the flash.*)
Absolutely fabulous!
(*The scene fades around* BUFFALO BILL, *who stands in the center, dizzily gripping his head.*

Scene 4

(*Dimly we see the* SENATORS *and* SITTING BULL'S INDIANS *glide back into view.*)
BUFFALO BILL
If it *please* the honorable senators . . . there is something I would like to say to *them*, as well.
(*Pause.*)
I wish to say . . . that there is far more at stake here, today, than the discovery of Indian grievances.
(*Pause.*)
At stake are these people's lives.
(*Pause.*)
In *some* ways, more than even that. For these are not just *any* Indians. These are *Sitting Bull's* Indians. . . . The last to surrender.
(*Pause.*)
The last of a kind.
(*Long pause.*)
So, in that way, you see, they are . . . perhaps more *important* for us than . . . any others.
(*Pause.*)
For it is we, alone, who have put them on this strip of arid land. And what becomes of them is . . . our responsibility.
(BUFFALO BILL *stares helplessly as the scene about him fades to black.*)

VOICE
And now, for your *pleasure*, BUFFALO BILL'S WILD WEST
SHOW *PROUDLY* PRESENTS . . .
(*Lights to black.*
Drum roll.)

Scene 5

(*Stage dark; drum roll continues. Weirdly colored spotlights begin to crisscross on the empty stage.*)

VOICE

THE MOST FEROCIOUS INDIAN ALIVE! . . .

(*The bars of a large round cage slowly emerge from the floor of the stage; then, around the bars, the Wild West Show fence seen earlier.*)

THE FORMER SCOURGE OF THE SOUTHWEST! . . .

(*The lights on the fence begin to glow; eerie, fantastical atmosphere.*

A tunnel-cage rolls out from the wings and connects with the large central cage.

Sound of an iron grate opening offstage.

Rodeo music up.)

The one 'n only . . . GERONIMO!

(*Enter* GERONIMO, *crawling through the tunnel; as soon as he is in sight, he stops, lifts his head, takes in his surroundings.*

Enter two COWBOY ROUSTABOUTS *with prods. They are enormous men—much larger than life-size. Their muscles bulge against their gaudy clothes. Their faces seem frozen in a sneer. Even their gun belts are oversized.*

They prod GERONIMO *along, raise the gate to the center cage and coax him in, closing it behind him. Then they move away.*

GERONIMO *paces about, testing the bars with his hands.*)
GERONIMO
I AM GERONIMO! WAR CHIEF OF THE GREAT CHIRI-
CAHUA APACHES!
(*He stalks about.*)
Around my neck is a string of white men's genitals! MEN I
HAVE KILLED! . . . Around my waist, the scalplocks of
white women's genitals! WOMEN I RAPED AND KILLED!
. . . *No Indian has ever killed or raped more than I!* Even the
Great Spirits cannot count the number! . . . My body is
painted with blood! I am red from white men's BLOOD! . . .
NO ONE LIVES WHO HAS KILLED MORE WHITE MEN
THAN I!
(BUFFALO BILL, *in his fancy buckskin, enters unnoticed by*
GERONIMO; *drum roll. He opens the cage door and walks inside.*
Once inside, he closes the door and stands still. GERONIMO
*senses his presence and stops moving. Lifts up his head as if to
hear better. Sniffs. Turns. Stares at* BUFFALO BILL.
Slowly, BUFFALO BILL *walks toward him. He stops just short
of the Indian. Then defiantly turns his back.*
GERONIMO *practically frothing.*
Long pause. GERONIMO *does nothing.*
BUFFALO BILL *walks calmly away, opens the cage door, and
exits. Disappears into the shadows.*
GERONIMO *stands trembling with frenzy.*
Lights fade to black.)

Scene 6

(*Lights up on the Senate Committee,* SITTING BULL'S INDIANS, *and* BUFFALO BILL.)

SENATOR LOGAN

Mister Grass, I wonder if you could be a bit more *specific* and tell us *exactly* what you think the Great Father has promised which he has not given.

JOHN GRASS

He promised to give us *as much as we would need, for as long as we would need it!*

SENATOR DAWES

Where did he promise you *that?*

JOHN GRASS

In a treaty.

SENATOR LOGAN

What treaty?

JOHN GRASS

A treaty signed some years ago, maybe five or six.

SENATOR LOGAN

Mister Grass, many treaties were signed five or six years ago. But frankly, I've never heard of an arrangement quite like that one.

JOHN GRASS

You took the Black Hills from us in this treaty!

SENATOR DAWES

You mean we *bought* the Black Hills in it!

(LOGAN *glares at* DAWES.)

JOHN GRASS

I have nothing else to say.

(*He turns and starts to walk away.*)

SENATOR LOGAN

Mister Grass! The . . . Senator . . . *apologizes* for his . . . tone.

(*Pause.* JOHN GRASS *returns.*)

JOHN GRASS

If you *bought* the Black Hills from us, where is our money?

SENATOR LOGAN

The money is in trust.

JOHN GRASS

Trust?

SENATOR MORGAN

He means, it's in a bank. Being *held* for you in a . . . bank. In *Washington!* Very . . . fine bank.

JOHN GRASS

Well, we would rather hold it ourselves.

SENATOR DAWES

The Great Father is worried that you've not been educated enough to spend it *wisely*. When he feels you have, you will receive every last penny of it. *Plus interest.*

(JOHN GRASS *turns in fury;* LOGAN *totally exasperated with* DAWES.)

BUFFALO BILL

Mister Grass, *please!* These men have come to *help* you! But their ways are *different* from yours; you must be *patient* with them.

JOHN GRASS

You said you would bring us the Great Father.

BUFFALO BILL

I *tried!* I *told* you! But he wouldn't come; *what else could I do?*

JOHN GRASS

You told us he was your *friend*.

BUFFALO BILL
HE *IS* MY FRIEND! *Look, don't you understand?* These men
are your *only* hope. If you turn away from them, it's like . . .
committing suicide.
(*Pause.*)
JOHN GRASS
(*To the* SENATORS.)
At Fort Laramie, Fort Lyon, and Fort Rice we signed treaties,
parts of which have never been fulfilled.
SENATOR DAWES
Which parts have never been fulfilled?
JOHN GRASS
At Fort Rice the Government advised us to be at *peace,* and
said that *if we did so,* we would receive a span of horses, five
bulls, ten chickens, and a wagon!
SENATOR LOGAN
You . . . really believe . . . these things were in the treaty?
JOHN GRASS
We were told they were.
SENATOR LOGAN
You . . . saw them written?
JOHN GRASS
We cannot read very well, but we were *told* they were!
(*The* SENATORS *glance sadly at one another.* JOHN GRASS *grows
confused. Pause.*)
We were also . . . promised a STEAMBOAT!
SENATOR MORGAN
A *steamboat?*
SENATOR DAWES
What in God's name were you supposed to do with a steamboat
in the middle of the plains?
(*He laughs.*)
JOHN GRASS
I don't know.
(*He turns in confusion and stares at* BUFFALO BILL; BUFFALO
BILL *turns helplessly to the* SENATORS. *As——*

Lights begin to fade.)
SITTING BULL
Where is the Great Father, Cody? . . . The one you said would help us. . . . The one you said you knew *so well*.
(*As lights go to black, a Mozart minuet is heard.*)

Scene 7

(*Lights up on White House Ballroom, in the center of which is a makeshift stage. The front drop of this stage is a melo-dramatic western-heroic poster with* "Scouts of the Plains, *by NED BUNTLINE*" *painted over it.*

The Mozart stops as——

A Negro USHER *enters.*)

USHER

This way, Mister President.

OL' TIME PRESIDENT

(*Offstage.*)

Thank you, George.

(*Enter the* OL' TIME PRESIDENT *in white tie and tails, cigar in mouth, brandy glass in hand.*)

This way, dear. They're about to start.

(*Enter the* FIRST LADY *in a formal gown.*)

FIRST LADY

Oh, this *is* exciting! Our *first real cowboys!*

(*The* USHER *leads them toward a pair of Louis XIV chairs set facing the stage. Drum roll.*)

OL' TIME PRESIDENT

Sssh. Here we go.

(*They sit.*

Enter, from behind the canvas drop, NED BUNTLINE. *He wears an exaggerated version of a plainsman's outfit.*)

NED BUNTLINE
Mister President, hon'rable First Lady,
Before you stands a character most shady,
A knave whose presence darkens this bright earth,
More than does the moon's eclipsing girth.
What's that you say, I'm rude to filth espouse,
When I'm the guest of such a clean, white house?
Fear not, there's somethin' I didn't mention:
Recently, I found redemption.
Ah, forgive me, I'm sorry, Ned Buntline's the name,
It's me who's brought Bill Cody fame.
Wrote twenty-seven books with him the hero.
Made 'm better known than Nero.
And though we sold 'em cheap, one for a dime,
The two of us was rich in no time.
As for my soul's redemption, it came thus:
I saw the nation profit more than us.
For with each one o' my excitin' stories,
Cody grew t' represent its glories.
Also helped relieve its conscience,
By showing pessimism's nonsense.
Later, when people asked t' *see* 'm,
I wrote a play for him to be in;
A scene of which we now perform for you,
As you've so graciously implored us to.

Cody, of course, impersonates himself,
As does Yours Truly.
The Crow Maiden is Italian actress
Paula Monduli.
Our evil Pawnee Chief, the great German actor
Gunther Hookman.
Our other Indians, I'm afraid,
Come from Brooklyn.
However, as a special treat tonight,
A visitor is here,
And I've added some new dialogue,
So he might appear.
Realize though, this man's come as Cody's friend,
He's not an actor.
Though of course in *my* play, who men *are*
Is the real factor.
So get set then for anything,
May the script be damned,
An' let's give Cody an' Wild Bill Hickok
A ROUSING HAND!
(*The* FIRST LADY *and the* OL' TIME PRESIDENT *applaud enthusiastically.* BUNTLINE *exits.*

The canvas drop is rolled up to reveal another canvas drop—a painted forest of the worst melodramatic order.

On stage, wooden as only the worst amateur actors can be, stand CODY *and* HICKOK, *the latter with long, glorious hair, fancy buckskin leggings, two large guns and a knife in his belt.*)

BUFFALO BILL
God pray we're in time. Those Pawnee devils will do anything.
(*Silence.*)

BUNTLINE
(*Prompting from offstage.*)
Especially . . .
(*Silence.*)

BUFFALO BILL
Think that's your line, Bill.

WILD BILL HICKOK
Oh, hell's thunder.
(*To* BUNTLINE.)
Better give it-a-me agin.

BUNTLINE
Especially . . .

HICKOK
Especially.

BUNTLINE
. . . at their . . .

HICKOK
At their.

BUFFALO BILL
(*Sotto voce.*)
. . . dreadful annual . . .

HICKOK
Dreadful. Annual.

BUNTLINE
. . . Festival of the Moon.

HICKOK
Festival of the Moon. Which is . . . 'bout t' happen. As it does
every . . .
(*Silence.*)

BUFFALO BILL
. . . year.

HICKOK
Year.

BUNTLINE
Very good.

HICKOK
Very good.

BUNTLINE
No!

HICKOK
Whose line's that?

BUFFALO BILL
No one's. He was jus' congratulatin' you.

HICKOK
Oh, Will, fer pity's sake, le' me out o' this.

BUNTLINE
Ad lib!

BUFFALO BILL
Yes! Pray God we're in time to stop the Pawnee's dreadful Festival of the Moon so that I, the great Buffalo Bill, can once again——

HICKOK
Will, stop it! A man may need money, but no man needs it this bad.

(*Enter* BUNTLINE, *tap-dancing the sound of horse's hooves.*)

BUFFALO BILL
Hark! Ned Buntline approaches! One o' the finest sharpshooters o' the West!

HICKOK
(*Under his breath.*)
Couldn't hit a cow in the ass from two paces.

BUFFALO BILL
Who knows? Maybe *he* can help us in our dire strait.

HICKOK
Mister and Missus President, if you're still out there, believe me, I'm as plumb embarrassed by this dude-written sissyshit as you.

BUNTLINE
HAIL, BUFFALO BILL! Hail—uh—Wild Bill Hickok. What brings you to this unlikely place?

HICKOK
Good fuckin' question.

BUNTLINE
Could it be that you seek, as I do, the camp of Uncas, evil Pawnee chief?

BUFFALO BILL
Yes, verily. We seek his camp so that I, the great Buffalo Bill,
can, once again, save someone in distress.
(HICKOK *groans.*)
This time, specifically, a virgin maiden——
HICKOK
You gotta be jokin'.
BUFFALO BILL
Will you shut up! Named Teskanjavila! Who, 'less I save her,
faces torture, sacrifice, and certain violations.
BUNTLINE
This bein' so, *let us join forces!*
HICKOK
Boy, where's your *self-respect?*
BUNTLINE
(*Weakly.*)
And save this virgin together.
BUFFALO BILL
(*To* HICKOK.)
Will you leave me alone!
HICKOK
This ain't a *proper place* for a man t' be!
BUFFALO BILL
Well, I THINK IT *IS!* I think I'm doin' a lot o' good up here!
Entertainin' people! Makin' 'em *happy!* Showin' 'em the West!
Givin' 'em somethin' t' be *proud* of! *You* go spend your life in
Dodge City if you want! I got *bigger* things in mind!
(*Stunned pause.*)
BUNTLINE
(*Very sheepishly.*)
To repeat: let us join forces and save this virgin together.
HICKOK
Buntline, if these guns were loaded, I'd——
BUNTLINE
(*Cueing the actors offstage.*)
HARK! The maiden's name is called!

NUMEROUS VOICES
(*Offstage.*)
Teskanjavila!

BUNTLINE
We must be near the camp of Uncas.

BUFFALO BILL
Evil Pawnee chief.

HICKOK
I'm gettin' sick.

BUNTLINE
Let us, therefore, approach with caution.

BUFFALO BILL
Guns ready.

BUNTLINE
Ears open.

BUFFALO BILL
(*To* HICKOK.)
Mouths shut!

BUNTLINE
Eyes alert.

BUFFALO BILL
So that I, Buffalo Bill, may once aga——
(HICKOK *has walked over and is staring into his face.*)
Just *what are you doin'?*

HICKOK
What're *you* doin'?

BUFFALO BILL
I'm doin' what I'm doin', *that's* what I'm doin'!

HICKOK
(*To* BUNTLINE.)
Always was intelligent.

BUFFALO BILL
I am doin' what my country *wants!* WHAT MY BELOVED
COUNTRY *WANTS!*

HICKOK
(*To the First Family.*)
This . . . is . . . what you want?

FIRST LADY
Absolutely!

OL' TIME PRESIDENT
Best play I've seen in years!

(HICKOK, *staggered, sits down on the stage.*)

BUFFALO BILL
When a man has a talent, a *God*-given talent, I think it's his
godly duty t' make the most of it.

(*Applause from the First Family.* BUFFALO BILL *nods acknowledgment. To* HICKOK.)

Ya see, Bill, what you fail to understand is that I'm not being
false to what I *was*. I'm simply *drawin'* on what I was . . .
and raisin' it to a higher level.

(*He takes a conscious pause.*)

Now. On with the show!

(*He points to* BUNTLINE, *cueing him to give the next line.*)

BUNTLINE
AVAST, AHOY! Above yon trees see the pale moon rising!

(*A cardboard moon is pulled upwards.*)

Feel the black night envelop us like a dark dream.

(BUNTLINE *and* CODY *shiver.*)

Sounds of the savage forest are heard. . . . We approach on
tiptoes.

BUFFALO BILL
(*To the First Family.*)

God pray we're in time.

(*They drop to their bellies as the canvas drop is raised to
reveal the camp of* UNCAS. *Tied to a totem pole is* TESKANJAVILA,
writhing sensually.

Clearly phony INDIANS *dance around her to the beat of drums.
The heroes crawl slowly forward.* HICKOK, *eyeing the girl lust-
fully, joins in.*)

FIRST LADY
That Hickok's rather handsome, isn't he?

OL' TIME PRESIDENT
I'm watching the girl. Note her legs. How white they are. For
an Indian. One can almost see the soft inner flesh of her thighs.

FIRST LADY
This play excites me!

OL' TIME PRESIDENT
We really should have more things like this at the White House.
(*The drums grow wilder. The* INDIANS *scream;* BUNTLINE, CODY, *and* HICKOK *invade the Indian camp site. Gunshots.* INDIANS *fall dead.*)

TESKANJAVILA
(*Italian accent.*)
Saved! A maiden's prayers are answered! And may I say, not a bit too soon! Already, my soft thighs had been pried open; my budding breasts pricked by the hot tip of an Indian spear. Yet, through it all, my maidenhead stayed secure. Here. In this pouch. Kept in this secret pocket. Where no one thought to look. Thus is innocence preserved! May Nazuma, God of Thunder, grant me happiness!
(*Thunder heard.*)

HICKOK
Buntline write that speech?

BUFFALO BILL
I think she changed it a little.
(UNCAS *rises from the dead.*)

UNCAS
(*German accent.*)
I am Uncas, Chief of the Pawnee Indians, recently killed for my lustful ways. Yet, before the white men came and did me in, I had this vision: the white man is great, the red man nothing. So, if a white man kills a red man, we must forgive him, for God intended man to be as great as possible, and by eliminating the inferior, the great man carries on God's work. Thus, the Indian is in no way wronged by being murdered. Indeed, quite the opposite: being murdered is his purpose in life. This was my recent vision. Which has brought light to the darkness of my otherwise useless soul. . . . And now, I die again.
(*He collapses.*)

HICKOK
Buntline write that?

BUFFALO BILL
Think Hookman changed it also. They all do it. It's our style. I dunno, people seem to like it.

HICKOK
Yeah? Well then, guess it mus' be my turn!
(*He pulls out his bowie knife.*)

BUFFALO BILL
HEY!

HICKOK
Make one false move an' I'll rip you 'part, friend or no.

BUNTLINE
Bill, look——

HICKOK
As for you, Buntline, you fangless lizard, you harmless bull, you ball of——

BUNTLINE
BRING DOWN THE CURTAIN!

HICKOK
First one touches that curtain, I cuts int' mincemeat an' eats fer dinner, *raw!*

FIRST LADY
I'm trembling all over.

HICKOK
Okay, Buntline. Now we're gonna settle up the score.

BUNTLINE
Score?

HICKOK
Men jus' don' humiliate Wil' Bill Hickok.

BUNTLINE
Hu—humiliate?

HICKOK
Or leastways don' do it twice, bein' dead shortly after the first occasion.

BUNTLINE
Wh—what . . . 're you talkin' about?

HICKOK
'Bout havin' to impersonate myself. 'Bout the humiliation o'
havin' to impersonate my *own personal self!*

BUNTLINE
Oh.

FIRST LADY
Fantastic!

BUNTLINE
Well, I dunno what t' say.

HICKOK
It weren't in the deal!

BUNTLINE
Deal?

HICKOK
You said if I came here, I could play Bat Masterson!

BUNTLINE
Ah, *that!*
(*He chuckles.*)
Well, . . . if you recall, I said *maybe* you could play Bat
Masterson. First, we had t' see how good you did as Hickok.

HICKOK
As *Hickok?* Chrissake, I AM Hickok!

BUNTLINE
Right.

HICKOK
Well, why in hell should I play *him* then?

BUNTLINE
Well, there's audience appeal.

FIRST LADY
There sure is!

BUNTLINE
BILL! Now—now, wait-a-second! Let's talk this over. Like
gentlemen.

BUFFALO BILL
Yeah. Right. Let's . . . not get too . . . carried away. After
all——

HICKOK

If you don' stay out o' this, I'm gonna slit yer stuffin' gizzard an' extract, inch by inch, what's guts in most folks, but in you is thorou' garbage.

BUFFALO BILL

Now wait-a-minute! Hold on! You—you think I'm jus' gonna stand here an'——

HICKOK

Oh, shut up! Dumb, dudelickin' FRAUD!

BUFFALO BILL

What?

HICKOK

If I gotta play Hickok, I'm gonna play Hickok the way Hickok should be *played!*

BUNTLINE

Put that knife away, please! . . . For godsakes. Cody, HELP ME! Cody!

(BUNTLINE *falls, a knife in his back. He crawls off the front of the stage; collapses.*)

FIRST LADY

He looks kind o' dead.

(BUFFALO BILL *heads for the body, stunned.*)

HICKOK

Sorry, Will. Guess I just ain't used to show business yet.

(*He chuckles and turns his attention to* TESKANJAVILA. BUFFALO BILL *is feeling for* BUNTLINE'S *pulse.*)

TESKANJAVILA

O, *Sancta Maria,* I don' like this gleam in his eye.

HICKOK

(*Striking a pose.*)

       Hail, sweet cookie, tart of tempting flavors,
       Why've I been denied your spicy favors?

TESKANJAVILA

AH! *What're you doing? HELP!*

(HICKOK *unties her from the pole, at the same time unhooking his gun belt. He works rapidly.*

BUFFALO BILL *lets* BUNTLINE'*s limp arm drop. He stares back at the stage, stunned.*)

FIRST LADY

Ooooh, look what he's doing now!

(*The First Family climb on the stage, the Negro* USHERS *bringing their chairs for them so they can have a more comfortable view.*)

Really, we must invite this theatre crowd more often.

(HICKOK *is now standing above* TESKANJAVILA, *who lies helpless at his feet.* BUFFALO BILL *watches from offstage, outside the ring. Also helpless.*)

HICKOK

Hickok, fastest shooter in the West, 'cept for Billy the Kid, who ain't as accurate; Hickok, deadliest shooter in the West, 'cept for Doc Holliday, who wields a sawed-off shotgun, which ain't fair; Hickok, shootinest shooter in the West, 'cept for Jesse James, who's absolutely indiscriminate; this Hickok, strong as an eagle, tall as a mountain, swift as the wind, fierce as a rattlesnake—a legend in his own time, or any other—this Hickok stands now above an Indian maiden——

TESKANJAVILA

I'm not an Indian and I'm not a maiden!

HICKOK

Who's not an Indian and not a maiden, but looks pretty good anyhow—an' asks those o' you watchin' t' note carefully the basic goodness of his very generous intentions, since otherwise . . .

(*He starts to finger her clothing.*)

. . . they might be mistaken for . . .

(*He rips open her buckskin dress.*)

. . . LUST!

(*She is left in a frilly Merry Widow corset.*)

TESKANJAVILA

Eh, bambino. If you don' mind, I'd like a little privacy.

(*To the First Family.*)

After all, I've not rehearsed this.

(HICKOK *pulls the cord, lowering the curtain.*)

OL' TIME PRESIDENT
Good show, Cody! *Good show!*

(BUFFALO BILL, *in a daze, walks to the stage and opens the curtain.*

"Scouts of the Plains" *drop seen. He stares at it. Pulls it down.*
NO ONE THERE.

Mozart minuet heard.

He looks around in total confusion.

The stage and all the White House furniture begin to disappear.

Lights fade to black, BUFFALO BILL *spinning dizzily in the middle.*

Music fades.)

Scene 8

(*Lights up again on the Senate Committee.*)

SENATOR LOGAN

Mister Grass. Let's leave aside the question of the steamboat. You mentioned the treaty at Fort Lyon and said that parts of that treaty had never been fulfilled. Well, I happen to be quite familiar with that particular treaty and happen to know that it is the Indians who did not fulfill its terms, not us.

JOHN GRASS

We did not *want* the cows you sent!

SENATOR LOGAN

You signed the treaty.

JOHN GRASS

We did not understand that we were to give up part of our reservation in exchange for these cows.

SENATOR DAWES

Why'd you think we were giving you twenty-five thousand cows?

JOHN GRASS

We were hungry. We thought it was for food.

SENATOR LOGAN

It wasn't explained that *only* if you gave us part of your reservation would you receive these cows?

JOHN GRASS

Yes. That was explained.

SENATOR MORGAN
And yet, you thought it was a gift.

JOHN GRASS
Yes.

SENATOR LOGAN
In other words, you thought you could have both the cows and the land?

JOHN GRASS
Yes.

SENATOR DAWES
Even though it was explained that you couldn't.

JOHN GRASS
Yes.

SENATOR MORGAN
This is quite hard to follow.

SENATOR LOGAN
Mister Grass, tell me, which would you prefer, cows or land?

JOHN GRASS
We prefer them both.

SENATOR LOGAN
Well, what if you can't have them both?

JOHN GRASS
We prefer the land.

SENATOR LOGAN
Well then, if you knew you had to give up some land to get these cows, why did you sign the treaty?

JOHN GRASS
The white men made our heads dizzy, and the signing was an accident.

SENATOR LOGAN
An accident?

JOHN GRASS
They talked in a threatening way, and whenever we asked questions, shouted and said we were stupid. Suddenly, the Indians around me rushed up and signed the paper. They were like men stumbling in the dark. I could not catch them.

SENATOR LOGAN
But you signed it, too.
(*Long pause.*)
SENATOR DAWES
Mister Grass. Tell me. Do the Indians really expect to keep all
this land and yet do nothing toward supporting themselves?
JOHN GRASS
We do not have to support ourselves. The Great Father prom-
ised to give us everything we ever needed; for that, we gave
him the Black Hills.
SENATOR LOGAN
Mister Grass. Which do you prefer—to be self-sufficient or to
be given things?
JOHN GRASS
We prefer them both.
SENATOR DAWES
Well, you can't *have* them both!
BUFFALO BILL
Please!
JOHN GRASS
I only know what we were promised.
SENATOR DAWES
That's *not* what you were promised!
JOHN GRASS
We believe it is.
BUFFALO BILL
What's going on here?
SENATOR MORGAN
Mister Grass. Wouldn't you and your people like to live like
the white man?
JOHN GRASS
We are happy like the Indian!
SENATOR LOGAN
He means, you wouldn't like to see your people made *greater*,
let's say?

JOHN GRASS

That is not possible! The Cheyenne and the Sioux are as great as people can be, already.

SENATOR MORGAN

Extraordinary, really.

BUFFALO BILL

Mister Grass. Surely . . . *surely* . . . your people would like to *improve their condition!*

JOHN GRASS

We would like what is owed us! If the white men want to give us more, that is fine also.

SENATOR LOGAN

Well, we'll see what we can do.

SENATOR MORGAN

Let's call the next. This is getting us nowhere.

JOHN GRASS

We would especially like the money the Great Father says he is holding for us!

SENATOR DAWES

I'm afraid that may be difficult, since, in the past, we've found that when an Indian's been given money, he's spent it all on liquor.

JOHN GRASS

When he's been given money, it's been so little there's been little else he could buy.

SENATOR MORGAN

Whatever, the Great Father does not like his Indian children getting drunk!

JOHN GRASS

Then tell the Great Father, who says he wishes us to live like white men, that when an Indian gets drunk, he is merely imitating the white men he's observed!

(*Laughter from the* INDIANS. LOGAN *raps his gavel.*)

SENATOR DAWES

STOP IT!

(*No effect.* LOGAN *raps more.*)
What in God's name do they think we're doing here? STOP IT!
(*Over the* INDIANS' *noise, the noise of a Wild West Show is heard; lights fade to black.*)

Scene 9

(*Wild West Show music and crisscrossing multicolored spotlights. The rodeo ring rises from the stage, its lights glittering. Wild West Show banners descend above the ring.*)

VOICE

And now, ladies and gentlemen, let's hear it for Buffalo Bill's fantastic company of authentic western heroes . . . the fabulous ROUGHRIDERS OF THE WORLD!

(*Enter, on heroically artificial horses, the* ROUGHRIDERS—*themselves heroically oversized.*

They gallop about the ring in majestic, intricate formation, whoopin' and shootin' as they do.)

With the ever-lovely . . . ANNIE OAKLEY!

(ANNIE OAKLEY *performs some startling trick shots as the others ride in circles about her.*)

And now, once again, here he is—the star of our show, the Ol' Scout himself; I mean the indestructible and ever-popular——

(*Drum roll.*)

——BUFFALO BILL!

(*Enter, on horseback,* BUFFALO BILL. *He is in his Wild West finery.*

He tours the ring in triumph while his ROUGHRIDERS *ride after him, finally exiting to leave him in the center, alone.*)

BUFFALO BILL

THANK YOU, THANK YOU! A *GREAT* show lined up tonight! With all-time favorite Johnny Baker, Texas Jack and his

twelve-string guitar, the Dancin' Cavanaughs, Sheriff Brad
and the Deadwood Mail Coach, Harry Philamee's Trained
Prairie Dogs, the Abilene County Girls' School Trick Roping
and Lasso Society, Pecos Pete and the——
VOICE
Bill.
BUFFALO BILL
(*Startled.*)
Hm?
VOICE
Bring on the Indians.
BUFFALO BILL
What?
VOICE
The *Indians.*
BUFFALO BILL
Ah.
(BUFFALO BILL *looks uneasily toward the wings as his company
of* INDIANS *enters solemnly and in ceremonial warpaint; they
carry the Sun Dance pole. At its summit is a buffalo skull.*)
And now, while my fabulous company of authentic . . .
American Indians go through the ceremonial preparations of
the Sun Dance, which they will re-create in all its death-defy-
ing goriness—let's give a warm welcome back to a courageous
warrior, the magnificent Chief Joseph——
(*Some* COWBOY ROUSTABOUTS *set up an inverted tub; music for*
CHIEF JOSEPH'*s entrance.*)
——who will recite his . . . celebrated speech. CHIEF JO-
SEPH!
(*Enter* CHIEF JOSEPH, *old and hardly able to walk.*)
CHIEF JOSEPH
In the moon of the cherries blossoming, in the year of our sur-
render, I, Chief Joseph, and what remained of my people, the
Nez Percés, were sent to a prison in Oklahoma, though General
Howard had promised we could return to Idaho, where we'd
always lived. In the moon of the leaves falling, still in the year

of our surrender, William Cody came to see me. He was a nice
man. With eyes that seemed . . . frightened; I . . . don't
know why. He told me I was courageous and said he admired
me. Then he explained all about his Wild West Show, in which
the great Sitting Bull appeared, and said if I agreed to join,
he would have me released from prison, and see that my people
received food. I asked what I could do, as I was not a very good
rider or marksman. And he looked away and said, "Just repeat,
twice a day, three times on Sundays, what you said that afternoon when our army caught you at the Canadian border, where
you'd been heading, and where you and your people would
have all been safe." So I agreed. For the benefit of my
people. . . . And for the next year, twice a day, three times
on Sundays, said this to those sitting around me in the dark,
where I could not see them, a light shining so brightly in my
eyes!
(*Pause.*

He climbs up on the tub.

Accompanied by exaggerated and inappropriate gestures.)
"Tell General Howard I know his heart. I am tired of fighting.
Our chiefs have been killed. Looking Glass is dead. The old
men are all dead. It is cold and we have no blankets. The children are freezing. My people, some of them, have fled to the
hills and have no food or warm clothing. No one knows where
they are—perhaps frozen. I want to have time to look for my
children and see how many of them I can find. Maybe I shall
find them among the dead. Hear me, my chiefs. I am tired. My
heart is sick and sad. From where the sun now stands, I will
fight no more forever. . . . "
(*He climbs down from the tub.*)
After which, the audience always applauded me.
(*Exit* CHIEF JOSEPH. *Pause.*)

     BUFFALO BILL
The Sun Dance . . . was the one religious ceremony common
to all the tribes of the plains. The Sioux, the Crow, the Black-

An Absolutely Original and Her

The Only One which Kings, Chief Rulers, Famous Generals, Nobles and the Most Illustrious and Enlightened Men of
Theme of Artistic, Poetic and Historic Inspiration. Which of All the Millions It has Entertained, Taught and Tra

COL. CODY'S ONLY CARD
TO THE PUBLIC.

"Wild West and
Congress of Rough Riders
of the World"

W. F. CODY
"BUFFALO BILL"

If Any Seek to Imitate It, They Defraud	It Controls All the Genuine Material of Its
If Any Claim to Rival It, They Falsify	It Alone Commands the Confidence of Potentates ▸ P
If Any Copy Its Announcements, It Is Forgery	It Is the Only Exhibition with which Governments Co-op

THE ONLY EXHIBITION IN ALL THE WORLD THAT I

READ THESE MEMORABLE WORD

"BILLY; FOR MY CHILDREN AND GRANDCHILDREN, WHO CA

BUFFALO
WILD

LADIES AND GENTLEMEN: PERMIT ME TO
INTRODUCE TO YOU
A CONGRESS OF ROUGH
RIDERS OF THE
WORLD"

BIL
WI

CONGRESS OF ROUGH RIDERS OF THE WO

OF ITS KIND THE FIRST, THE ONLY, AND THE LAST, IT IS A REVELATION
THE MOST COLOSSAL AND THE STRANGEST ENTERTAINMENT EVER ORGANIZED OR DREAMED OF.

The Only Object Teacher History has Ever Had, or Recreation Furnished.
Whatever Others May Say or Care, to Whole World Pronounces it Supremely and Uniquely Great.
The Mirror of American Manhood. The Camp of the Makers of a Nation's History.

Prompted by Kings, Honored by Nations. A Paragon at Home, a Triumph Abroad.
Rough Riders Schooled to Hardship, and to Whom the Saddle is an Heirloom.
An Equine and Equestrian Study, with Horse and Man a Sculptor's Same Ideal.

Hazardous Pastimes of which the Great Plains and Deserts are the Natural Playground.

A HOLIDAY REFLECTING YEARS OF ROMANCE
AND THE REALITY OF IMPERISHABLE DEEDS.
FEATS OF FEARLESS SKILL, FASHIONED BY NECESSITY,
PERFECTED IN DANGER, AND CROWNED BY VICTORY.
THE ONE PRESENTMENT OF GRIM-VISAGED WAR BEFORE THE STARTLED FACE OF SMILING PEACE.
MAKING THE NEW WORLD AND THE OLD APPEAR IN
BRAVEST AND MOST BRILLIANT RIVALRIES
ITSELF A NOBLE PART OF WHAT IT SHOWS, WHICH OFTEN SEEN THE MORE ATTRACTIVE GROWS.

Enterprise of Inimitable Lustre.

To America and Americans

Than Historic: It Is History Itself in Living Lessons
e Imitations of Fancy, but the Stupendous Realism of Facts
Speculation of Apes, but an Institution of Heroes

NOT AN EMPTY CHEATING ECHO, BUT DARING DEEDS INCARNATE
TELLING ITS THRILLING TALES WITH RIFLE, SWORD and SPEAR
USING IN PLACE OF HALTING WORDS INSPIRING, SPLENDID, ACTION

COUNTERPART. EXCLUSIVELY ITS OWN CREATION.

NERAL SHERMAN TO COL. CODY,

ER SEE THESE THINGS AS WE SAW THEM, I THANK YOU."

ITS GREAT ORIGINATOR NOW RIDES ALONE UPON FAME'S WARPATH

THE LAST IN SERVICE OF THE GREATER SCOUTS TO WHOM OUR ARMY'S SAFETY WAS ENTRUSTED.

The Master Horseman, More Picturesque and Perfect than Alexander or Bucephalus.
Commanding the Grand Head of All the World's Most Noted Riders.
No Toppling Tents Could Cover Such An Equestrian Gathering of Nations.

No Hundred Theatres Combined Inclose Its Proud Reviews and Battle Spectacles.
The Plains, the Steppes, the Pampas, Are Its Platform.
The Free Range of the Open Air, the Coliseum Nature Builds for It.

Among Its Features, Martial Pageants, Dazzling Reviews, Savage Displays of Fearful War and Foray.

Wild & Most Wondrous Riders on Naked Steeds
STRANGE AND EXCITING NOMADIC RACES.

THE REGULAR CAVALRY OF MANY FLAGS.   DESERT-BORN BEDOUINS IN AMAZING FEATS
THE THRILLING EPISODES, STRUGGLES, ESCAPES, ADVENTURES, MARKSMANSHIP AND UNIQUE PASTIMES OF BORDER LIFE.

REGULAR ARTILLERY JUST AS IN ACTION
THE WARLIKE ACTS AND ARMS OF MANY LANDS.
NOT ONE OF WHICH CAN EVER ELSEWHERE BE PRODUCED OR DUPLICATED

feet, the Kiowa, the Blood, the Cree, the Chippewa, the Arapaho, the Pawnee, the Cheyenne. It was *their* way of proving they were . . . real Indians.
(*Pause.*)
The bravest would take the ends of long leather thongs and hook them through their chest muscles, then, pull till they'd ripped them out. The greater the pain they could endure, the greater they felt the Spirits would favor them. Give them what they needed. . . . Grant them . . . salvation.
(*Pause.*)
Since the Government has officially outlawed this ritual, we will merely imitate it.
(*Pause.*)
And no one . . . will be hurt.
(*He steps back.*

The dance begins. The INDIANS *take the barbed ends of long leather thongs that dangle from the top of the Sun Dance pole and hook them through plainly visible chest harnesses. Then they pull back against the center and dance about it, flailing their arms and moaning as if in great pain.*

Suddenly JOHN GRASS *enters.* A ROUSTABOUT *tries to stop him.*

The INDIANS *are astonished to see this intruder;* BUFFALO BILL *stunned.*

JOHN GRASS *pulls the* INDIANS *out of their harnesses, rips open his shirt, and sticks the barbs through his chest muscles.*

He chants and dances. The other INDIANS, *realizing what he's doing, blow on reed whistles, urge him on. Finally he collapses, blood pouring from his chest.*

The INDIANS *gather around him in awe.*

BUFFALO BILL *walks slowly toward* JOHN GRASS; *stares down at him.*

The INDIANS *remove the Sun Dance pole and trappings.*

BUFFALO BILL *crouches and cradles* JOHN GRASS *in his arms.*

As lights fade to black.)

Scene 10

(*Light up on* WHITE HOUSE USHER.)

USHER

The President is exercising in the gym, sir. This way.

(*Enter* BUFFALO BILL.)

BUFFALO BILL

You're sure it's all right?

USHER

Yes, sir. He said to show you right in. Very pleased you're here. (*The* USHER *gestures for* CODY *to pass. When he does, the* USHER *bows, turns, and leaves.*

BUFFALO BILL *stops.*

Gym noise heard.

Lights up on the OL' TIME PRESIDENT, *dressed like* HICKOK *and astride a mechanical horse pushed by another* USHER. *Near him sits an old Victrola; "On the Old Chisholm Trail" is playing.*

The OL' TIME PRESIDENT *spurs his horse onwards.*

Nearby hangs a punching bag.

BUFFALO BILL *stares at the scene, stupefied; walks cautiously forward.*)

BUFFALO BILL

Uh——

OL' TIME PRESIDENT

Cody! My ol' buddy! Welcome back! Long time no see!

BUFFALO BILL

Yes, sir. Long time . . . no see.

OL' TIME PRESIDENT

Wha'd'ya think o' this thing? Latest in athletic equipment. Just got it yesterday.

BUFFALO BILL

It's a . . . nice imitation.

OL' TIME PRESIDENT

More power.

USHER

Pardon?

OL' TIME PRESIDENT

Little more power.

(*The* USHER *nods; the mechanical horse bounces faster.*)

Good for the figure, this bronco riding. GIDDYAP! You orn'ry sonofabitch.

(*He laughs; whips his horse furiously.*)

BUFFALO BILL

Sir. What I've come t' talk t' you about is very important.

OL' TIME PRESIDENT

Can't hear ya. Speak up!

BUFFALO BILL

(*Pointing to the phonograph.*)

May I turn this down?

OL' TIME PRESIDENT

Tell me. You think I look a little bit like Hickok?

BUFFALO BILL

Mr. President, would you *please stop this?*

OL' TIME PRESIDENT

What?

BUFFALO BILL

STOP THIS!!!

OL' TIME PRESIDENT

Whoa, Nellie.

USHER

Pardon?

OL' TIME PRESIDENT
WHOA, NELLIE!
(*The* USHER *stops the horse; shuts off the phonograph.*
Cold tone.)
All right. What is it?
BUFFALO BILL
Well sir, I'm here t' ask if you'd come with me t' Sitting Bull's reservation.
OL' TIME PRESIDENT
Whose reservation?
BUFFALO BILL
Sitting Bull's. He was in my Wild West Show for a time. And naturally, I feel a sort o' . . . obligation.
(*Pause.*)
Personal . . . obligation.
OL' TIME PRESIDENT
I see.
BUFFALO BILL
I figure you're just about the only one left now who can really help him. His people are in a desperate way.
OL' TIME PRESIDENT
Tell me: this—uh—Sitting Bull. Isn't he the one who wiped out Custer?
BUFFALO BILL
Uh, well, yes, he . . . is, but it was, ya know, nothin'—uh—personal.
(*Weak laugh.*)
OL' TIME PRESIDENT
Can't help.
BUFFALO BILL
What?
OL' TIME PRESIDENT
I'm sorry, but I can't help.
BUFFALO BILL
You don't understand the *situation!*

OL' TIME PRESIDENT

I *don't?* All right, let's say I *want* to help. *What do I do for
'em?* Do I give 'em back their land? Do I resurrect the buffalo?

BUFFALO BILL

You can do *other* things!

OL' TIME PRESIDENT

No, Cody. *Other* people can do other things. *I* . . . must do
magic. Well, I can't *do* magic for *them;* it's too late.

BUFFALO BILL

I promised Sitting Bull you'd come.

OL' TIME PRESIDENT

Then you're a fool.

BUFFALO BILL

They're going to *die.*

(*Long pause.*)

OL' TIME PRESIDENT

Tell ya what. 'Cause I'm so *grateful* to you. . . . For your Wild
West Show. For what it's *done.* For this country's *pride,* its
glory.

(*Pause.*)

I'll do you a favor; I'll send a committee in my place.

BUFFALO BILL

A committee *won't be able to help!*

OL' TIME PRESIDENT

Oh, I think the gesture will mean something.

BUFFALO BILL

To WHOM?

(*Silence.*)

OL' TIME PRESIDENT

Being a great President, Cody, is like being a great eagle. A
great . . . *hunted* eagle. I mean, you've got to know . . .
when t' stay put.

(*He smiles.*)

On your way out, Bill, tell the guards, no more visitors today,
hm?

(*He nods to the* USHER, *who starts to rock him again.*
As BUFFALO BILL *slowly leaves.*
Music back up.
Lights fade to black.)

Scene 11

(*Lights up on reservation, as when last seen.*

The INDIANS *are laughing; the* SENATORS, *rapping for silence.*)

SENATOR DAWES

What in God's name do they think we're doing here?

BUFFALO BILL

(*To* SITTING BULL.)

Please! You must tell them to stop this *noise!*

SITTING BULL

You told us you would bring the Great Father.

BUFFALO BILL

I told you! He couldn't come! It's not my fault! Besides, these men are the Great Father's representatives! Talking to them is like talking to him!

SITTING BULL

If the Great Father wants us to believe he is wise, why does he send us men who are *stupid?*

BUFFALO BILL

They're *not* stupid! They just don't see things the way *you* do!

SITTING BULL

Yes. Because they are stupid.

BUFFALO BILL

They're *not stupid!*

SITTING BULL

Then they must be blind. It is the only other explanation.

BUFFALO BILL
All right. Tell me. Do *you* understand them?

SITTING BULL
Why should I want to understand men who are stupid?

BUFFALO BILL
Because if you *don't,* your people will *starve to death.*
(*Long pause.*)
All right. . . . Now. Let me try to explain some . . . *basics.*
(*To the* SENATORS.)
Well, as you've just seen, the Indian can be hard t' figure.
What's one thing t' us is another t' him. For example, farmin'.
Now the *real* problem here is not poor soil. The real problem's
plowin'. Ya see, the Indian believes the earth is sacred and sees
plowin' as a sacrilegious act. Well, if ya can't get 'em t' plow,
how can ya teach 'em farmin'? Impossible. Fertile land's another problem. There just ain't much of it, an' what there is, the
Indians prefer to use for pony racin'. Naturally, it's been explained to 'em how people can race ponies anywhere, but they
prefer the fertile land. They say, if their ancestors raced ponies
there, that's where *they* must race. . . . Another difficult problem is land itself. The majority of 'em, ya see, don't understand
how land can be owned, since they believe the land was made
by the Great Spirits for the benefit of everyone. So, when we do
buy land from 'em, they think it's just some kind o' temporary
loan, an' figure we're kind o' foolish fer payin' good money for
it, much as someone 'ud seem downright foolish t' us who paid
money fer the sky, say, or the ocean. Which . . . causes
problems.
(*Pause.*)
Well, what I'm gettin' at is *this:* if *their* way o' seein' is hard
fer *us* t' follow, ours is just as hard fer *them.* . . . There's an
old Indian legend that when the first white man arrived, he
asked some Indians for enough land t' put his blanket down
onto fer the night. So they said yes. An' next thing they knew,
he'd unraveled this blanket till it was one long piece o' thread.
Then he laid out the thread, an' when he was done, he'd roped

off a couple o' square miles. Well, the Indian finds that sort o' behavior hard t' understand. That's all I have t' say. Maybe, if you think about it, some good'll finally come from all this. I dunno.

SENATOR MORGAN

Thank you. We *shall* think about it. And hope the Indians think about it, too. And cause no more disturbances like the one just now. . . . Ask Sitting Bull if he has anything to say.

BUFFALO BILL

Sitting Bull.

SITTING BULL

Of course I will speak if they desire me to. I suppose it is only such men as they desire who may say anything.

SENATOR LOGAN

Anyone here may speak. If you have something to say, we will listen. Otherwise, sit down.

SITTING BULL

Tell me, do you know who I am, that you talk as you do?

BUFFALO BILL

SITTING BULL, PLEASE!

(*Long pause.*)

SITTING BULL

I wish to say that I fear I spoke hastily just now. In calling you . . . stupid. For my friend William Cody tells me you are here with good intentions. So I ask forgiveness for my unthinking words, which might have caused you to wreak vengeance on my people for what was not their doing, but *mine, alone.*

SENATOR LOGAN

We are pleased you speak so . . . sensibly. You are . . . forgiven.

SITTING BULL

I shall tell you, then, what I want you to say to the Great Father for me. And I shall tell you everything that is in my heart. For I know the Great Spirits are looking down on me today and want me to tell you everything that is in my heart. For you are the only people now who can help us.

(*Pause.*)

My children . . . are dying. They have no warm clothes, and their food is gone. The old way is gone. No longer can they follow the buffalo and live where they wish. I have prayed to the Great Spirits to send us back the buffalo, but I have not yet seen any buffalo returning. So I know the old way is gone. I think . . . my children must learn a *new* way if they are to live. Therefore, tell the Great Father that if he wishes us to live like white men, we will do so.

(*Stunned reaction from his Indians. He silences them with a wave of his hand.*)

For I know that if that pleases him, we will benefit. I am looking always to the benefit of my children, and so, want only to please the Great Father. . . . Therefore, tell him for me that I have never yet seen a white man starving, so he should send us food so we can live like the white man, as he wants. Tell him, also, we'd like some healthy cattle to butcher—I wish to kill three hundred head at a time. For that is the way the white man lives, and we want to please the Great Father and live the same way. Also, ask him to send us each six teams of mules, because that is the way the white men make a living, and I want my children to make as good a living. I ask for these things only because I was advised to follow your ways. I do not ask for anything that is not needed. Therefore, tell him to send to each person here a horse and buggy. And four yokes of oxen and a wagon to haul wood in, since I have never yet seen a white man dragging wood by hand. Also, hogs, male and female, and male and female sheep for my children to raise from. If I leave anything out in the way of animals that the white men have, it is a mistake, for I want every one of them! For we are great Indians, and therefore should be no less great as white men. . . . Furthermore, tell him to send us warm clothing. And glass for the windows. And toilets. And clean water. And beds, and blankets, and pillows. And fur coats, and gloves. And hats. And *pretty silk ties*. As you see, I do not ask for anything that is not needed. For the Great Father has advised us to live like

white men, so clearly, this is how we should live. For it is your
doing that we are here on this reservation, and it is not right
for us to live in poverty. And be treated like beasts. . . . That
is all I have to say.

SENATOR LOGAN

I want to say something to that man before he sits down, and
I want all the Indians to listen very carefully to what I'm going
to tell him. . . . Sitting Bull, this committee invited you to
come here for a friendly talk. When you talked, however, you
insulted them. I understand this is not the first time you have
been guilty of such an offense.

SITTING BULL

Do you know who I am that you talk the way you do?

SENATOR LOGAN

I know you are Sitting Bull.

SITTING BULL

Do you really not recognize me? Do you really not know who
I am?

SENATOR LOGAN

I said, I know you are Sitting Bull!

SITTING BULL

You know I am Sitting Bull. But do you know what *position*
I hold?

SENATOR DAWES

We do not recognize any difference between you and other
Indians.

SITTING BULL

Then I will tell you the difference. So you will never ever make
this mistake again. I am here by the will of the Great Spirits,
and by their will I am a chief. My heart is red and sweet, and
I know it is sweet, for whatever I pass near tries to touch me
with its tongue, as the bear tastes honey and the green leaves
lick the sky. If the Great Spirits have chosen anyone to be
leader of their country, know that it is not the Great Father;
it is myself.

SENATOR DAWES
WHO IS THIS CREATURE?

SITTING BULL
I will show you.
(*He raises his hand. The* INDIANS *turn and start to leave.*)

SENATOR LOGAN
Just a minute, Sitting Bull!
(SITTING BULL *stops.*)
Let's get something straight. You said to this committee that you were chief of all the people of this country and that you were appointed chief by the Great Spirits. Well, I want to say that you were *not* appointed by the Great Spirits. Appointments are not made that way. Furthermore, I want to say that you are arrogant and stupidly proud, for you are not a great chief of this country or any other; that you have no following, no power, no control, and no right to any control.

SITTING BULL
I wish to say a word about my not being a chief, having no authority, being proud——

SENATOR LOGAN
You are on an Indian reservation merely at the sufferance of the Government. You are fed by the Government, clothed by the Government; your children are educated by the Government, and all you have and are today is because of the Government. I merely say these things to notify you that you cannot insult the people of the United States of America or its committees. And I want to say to the rest of you that you must learn that you are the equals of other men and must not let this one man lead you astray. You must stand up to him and not permit him to insult people who have come all this way just to help you. . . . That is all I have to say.

SITTING BULL
I wish to say a word about my not being a chief, having no authority, being proud, and considering myself a great man in general.

SENATOR LOGAN
We do not care to talk with you any more today.

SENATOR DAWES
Next Indian.

SITTING BULL
I said, I wish to speak about my having no authority, being not a chief, and——

SENATOR LOGAN
I said, we've heard enough of you today!
(SITTING BULL *raises his hand; the* INDIANS *leave.*

SITTING BULL *stares at* CODY.)

SITTING BULL
If a man is the chief of a great people, and has lived only for those people, and has done many great things for them, *of course he should be proud!*
(*He exits.*

Lights fade to black.)

Scene 12

(*Guitar heard:* "Chisholm Trail."
Lights up on saloon. Most of it is in shadows. Only a poker table is well lit.
A bar is in the distance.
Swinging doors.
Various COWBOYS *slouch about.*)

JESSE JAMES
(*Sings.*)
    Walkin' down the street in ol" Dodge City,
    Wherever I look things look pretty shitty.
        Coma ti yi youpy, youpy yea, youpy yea,
        Coma ti yi youpy, youpy yea.
    An' the very worst thing that I can see,
    Is a dead man walkin' straight toward me.
        Coma ti yi youpy, youpy yea, youpy yea,
        Coma ti yi youpy, youpy yea.
    This dead man clearly ain't feelin' well,
    If you ask me I think he's just found hell.
        Coma ti yi youpy, youpy yea, youpy yea,
        Coma ti yi youpy, you——
(*Enter* BUFFALO BILL *in an overcoat flecked with snow. Gloves.*
A warm scarf.)

BUFFALO BILL
Where's Hickok? I'm told Hickok's here. . . . *Where's Hickok?*

BILLY THE KID
Hey, uh . . . stranger.
(*He chuckles.*

Before he can draw, BUFFALO BILL *gets the drop on him.*)
BUFFALO BILL
Who're you?
PONCHO
He . . . is the original . . . Billy the Kid.
(JESSE JAMES *makes a move and* BUFFALO BILL *draws his other gun; gets the drop on him as well.*)
And *he* is the original Jesse James. The original Doc Holliday is, I'm afraid, out to lunch.
(*The* COWBOYS *move to encircle* BUFFALO BILL.)
Who're *you?*
BUFFALO BILL
Buffalo Bill.
PONCHO
Really?
(PONCHO *laughs. Enter* HICKOK.)
HICKOK
Cody! My ol' buddy!
(*They embrace.*)
Oh, great balls o' fire! What a surprise! Why jus' this mornin'
I was . . . was . . .
(*Pause.*)
picturin' you.
BUFFALO BILL
You were?
HICKOK
So how ya been? C'mon. Tell me.
BUFFALO BILL
Oh, I been . . . fine.
HICKOK
Great!
BUFFALO BILL
An' you?

HICKOK
Never better. *Never better!*

BUFFALO BILL
Mus' say, you've sure got some . . . famous . . . people here.
(*Slight laugh.*)

HICKOK
Well, ya know, it's . . . that kind o' place.
(*He laughs, too; slaps* CODY *on the back. He leads him to a table.*)
So! . . . Whatcha doin' here? Great honor. *Great honor!*

BUFFALO BILL
I hafta . . . *talk* . . . t' you.

HICKOK
Sure thing.
(*He waves the* COWBOYS *away; they sit at the table in privacy.*)

BUFFALO BILL
I've just come from Sitting Bull's reservation.

HICKOK
Oh?
(*Slight laugh.*)
That reservation's a far piece from here.

BUFFALO BILL
I need your help! Sitting Bull is . . .
(*Pause.*)

HICKOK
What?
(*Long silence.*)

BUFFALO BILL
I'm scared. . . . I dunno what's happenin' anymore. . . .
Things have gotten . . . *beyond* me.
(*He takes a drink.*)
I see them *everywhere.*
(*Weak smile; almost a laugh.*
Music.

INDIANS *appear in the shadows beyond the saloon.*)

In the grass. The rocks. The branches of dead trees.
(*Pause.*)
Took a drink from a river yesterday an' they were even there,
beneath the water, their hands reachin' up, I dunno whether
beggin', or t' . . . drag me under.
(*Pause.*)
I wiped out their food, ya see. . . . Didn't *mean* to, o' course.
(*He laughs to himself.*)
I mean IT WASN'T MY FAULT! The railroad men needed
food. They *hired* me t' *find* 'em food! Well. How was *I* t' know
the goddam buffalo reproduced so slowly? *How was I to know
that?* NO ONE KNEW THAT!
(*Pause.*

The INDIANS *slowly disappear.*)
Now, Sitting Bull is . . .
(*Long pause.*)
            HICKOK
What?
            BUFFALO BILL
The . . . hearing was a shambles. I brought these Senators,
you see. To Sitting Bull's reservation. It . . . was a shambles.
(*Pause.*)
So we left. He . . . *insulted* them.
(*Pause.*)
Then I saw the letter.
(*Silence.*)
            HICKOK
What letter?
            BUFFALO BILL
The letter to McLaughlin. The letter ordering . . . it to be
. . . done.
(*Pause.*)
So I rode back. Rode all night. Figuring, maybe . . . if I can
just *warn* him. . . . But the reservation soldiers stopped me
and . . . made me . . . drink with them. And by the time I
got there, he . . . was dead. The greatest Indian who'd ever

lived. Shot. By order of the Government. Shot with a Gatling gun.
(*Pause.*)
While the . . . wonderful, gray horse I'd given him for . . . appearing in my show danced his repertory of tricks in the background. Since a gunshot was his cue to perform.
(*He laughs.*
Stops.
Long silence.)

HICKOK

Well now. In exactly what way did you imagine *I* could . . . *help* this . . . situation?

BUFFALO BILL

You have what I *need* . . . now.

HICKOK

(*Smiling slightly.*)
Oh?

BUFFALO BILL

I'm *scared*, you see.
(*Pause.*)
Scared . . . not . . . so much of *dyin'*, but . . . dyin' *wrong*.
(*Slight laugh.*)
Dyin' . . . in the center of my arena with . . . makeup on.
(*Long pause.*)
Then I thought of you. . . . Remembered that night in the White House. Remembered thinking, "My God! Look at Hickok. Hickok *knows just who he is!*"
(*Pause.*)
"*Hickok has the answer*," I said. . . . Hickok knows who he *is*.
(*Pause.*)
I must see Hickok again.
(*Long silence.*)

HICKOK

Well I'm glad you came. Yes. Glad . . . to be able to . . . help.
(*Pause.*)

Funny. That night, in the White House, I remember thinking:
"My God, it's *Cody* who's got the answer!"

HICKOK

BUFFALO BILL

. . . What?

HICKOK

Poncho!

PONCHO

Si, señor.

HICKOK

Bring in our . . . um . . .

PONCHO

Ah! *Si, señor! Ahorita.*

(*Exit* PONCHO.)

HICKOK

Naturally, at first, you may be a bit startled. Put off. Not . . .
exactly . . . what you *had in mind.* Yet! I'm sure that once you
think about it, you'll agree *it's the only way.* Just like Jesse has.
Billy. Doc Holliday. The boys.

BUFFALO BILL

What are you talkin' about?

HICKOK

Why, takin' what you were and raisin' it to a . . . higher level.
(*He laughs.*)
Naturally, for my services, I get a small fee. Percentage. You
get 50 per cent right off the top. Of course, if at any time you
aren't happy, you can leave. Take your business elsewhere.
That's written in. Keeps us on our toes. Mind you, this . . .
enterprise . . . is still in its infancy. The *potential*, though
. . . is unlimited. For example, think of this. The *great national
good* . . . that could come from this: some of you, let's say,
would concentrate strictly on theatrics. MEANWHILE! *Others*
of you would concentrate on purely humanitarian affairs. Save
. . . well, not Sitting Bull, but . . . some Indian down in
Florida. Another up in Michigan. Perhaps expand into Canada.
Mexico. Central America. SOUTH AMERICA! My God, there

must be literally *millions* of people who could benefit by your presence! Your . . . *simultaneous presence!*

PONCHO

Here they are, *señor!*

(*Enter a group of men dressed as* BUFFALO BILL. *Their faces are covered by masks of his face. They wear his florid buckskin clothes—if anything, even more elaborately designed.*)

HICKOK

Naturally, we've still got a few wrinkles to iron out. Color of hair. Color of eyes. That sort of thing. But with *you* here, exercising artistic control, why, we could go on like this *forever!*

(BUFFALO BILL, *stunned by the sight, fires his guns at the duplicate Codys. They fall and immediately rise again.*

They slowly surround him.

He screams as he shoots.

They disappear.

The saloon fades to black.

BUFFALO BILL *alone on stage.*)

BUFFALO BILL

AND NOW TO CLOSE! AND *NOW TO CLOSE!*

VOICE

Not *yet.*

(*Pause.*)

They also killed the rest of his tribe.

(*Music.*

INDIANS *enter mournfully. They carry a large white sheet.*

Sound of wind.

BUFFALO BILL *watches, then moves slowly away; exits.*)

Scene 13

(The INDIANS *cover the center area with the huge white sheet, then lie down upon it in piles.*

Enter COLONEL FORSYTH, *a* LIEUTENANT, *and two* REPORTERS, *their coat collars turned up for the wind.* CODY *is with them; he carries a satchel.)*

FIRST REPORTER

Fine time of year you men picked for this thing.

COLONEL FORSYTH

They're heathens; they don't celebrate Christmas.

FIRST REPORTER

I don't mean the date, I mean the weather.

COLONEL

Uncomfortable?

FIRST REPORTER

Aren't you?

COLONEL

One gets used to it.

SECOND REPORTER

Colonel, I gather we lost twenty-nine men, thirty-three wounded. How many Indians were killed?

COLONEL

We wiped them out.

SECOND REPORTER
Yes, I know. But how many *is* that?

COLONEL
We haven't counted.

LIEUTENANT
The snow has made it difficult. It started falling right after the battle. The bodies were covered almost at once. By night they were frozen.

COLONEL
We more than made up for Custer, though, I can tell you that.

SECOND REPORTER
But Custer was killed fifteen years ago!

COLONEL
So what?

LIEUTENANT
If there are no more questions, we'll take you to——

FIRST REPORTER
I have one! Colonel Forsyth, some people are referring to your victory yesterday as a massacre. How do you feel about that?

COLONEL
One can always find someone who'll call an overwhelming victory a massacre. I suppose they'd prefer it if we'd let more of our own boys get shot!

FIRST REPORTER
Then you don't think the step you took was harsh?

COLONEL
Of course it was harsh. And I don't like it any more than you. But had we shirked our responsibility, skirmishes would have gone on for years, costing our country millions, as well as untold lives. Of course innocent people have been killed. In war they always are. And of course our hearts go out to the innocent victims of this. But war is not a game. It's tough. And demands tough decisions. In the long run I believe what happened here at this reservation yesterday will be justified.

FIRST REPORTER
Are you implying that the Indian Wars are finally over?

COLONEL

Yes, I believe they're finally over. This ludicrous buffalo religion of Sitting Bull's people was their last straw.

SECOND REPORTER

And now?

COLONEL

The difficult job of rehabilitating begins. But that's more up General Howard's line.

LIEUTENANT

Why don't we go and talk with him? He's in the temporary barracks.

COLONEL

He can tell you about our future plans.

(*They start to leave.*)

BUFFALO BILL

You said you'd——

LIEUTENANT

Ah, yes, it's that one.

(*He points to a body.*)

BUFFALO BILL

Thank you.

(*He stays. The others leave; he stares at the grave.* SITTING BULL *has entered, unnoticed.* BUFFALO BILL *takes a sprig of pine from the satchel and is about to put it on the grave.*)

SITTING BULL

Wrong grave. I'm over here. . . . As you see, the dead can be buried, but not so easily gotten rid of.

BUFFALO BILL

Why didn't you listen to me? I *warned* you what would happen! Why didn't you *listen?*

(*Long silence.*)

SITTING BULL

We had land. . . . You wanted it; you took it. That . . . I understand perfectly. What I cannot understand . . . is why you did all this, *and at the same time* . . . professed your love.

(*Pause.*)

BUFFALO BILL
Well . . . well, what . . . about *your* mistakes? *Hm?* For, for example: you were very unrealistic . . . about things. For . . . example: did you *really* believe the buffalo would return? *Magically* return?

SITTING BULL
It seemed no less likely than Christ's returning, and a great deal more useful. Though when I think of their reception here, I can't see why either would really want to come back.

BUFFALO BILL
Oh, God. Imagine. For awhile, I actually thought my Wild West Show would *help*. I could give you money. Food. Clothing. And also make people *understand* things . . . better.
(*He laughs to himself.*)
That was my reasoning. Or, anyway, *part* . . .
(*Pause.*)
of my reasoning.

SITTING BULL
(*Slight smile.*)
Your show was very popular.
(*Pause.*)

BUFFALO BILL
We had . . . *fun,* though, you and I.
(*Pause.*)
Didn't we?

SITTING BULL
Oh, yes. And that's the terrible thing. We had all surrendered. We were on reservations. We could not fight, or hunt. We could do nothing. Then you came and allowed us to imitate our glory. . . . It was humiliating! For sometimes, we could almost imagine it was *real.*

BUFFALO BILL
Guess it wasn't so authentic, was it?
(*He laughs slightly to himself.*)

SITTING BULL
How could it have been? You'd have killed all your performers in one afternoon.

(*Pause.*)

BUFFALO BILL

You know what worried me most? . . . The fear that I might die, in the middle of the arena, with all my . . . makeup on. *That* . . . is what . . . worried me most.

SITTING BULL

What worried *me* most . . . was something I'd said the year before. Without thinking.

BUFFALO BILL

(*Softly.*)

What?

SITTING BULL

I'd agreed to go onto the reservation. I was standing in front of my tribe, the soldiers leading us into the fort. And as we walked, I turned to my son, who was beside me. "Now," I said, "you will never know what it is to be an Indian, for you will never again have a gun or pony. . . ." Only later did I *realize* what I'd said. These things, the gun and the pony—they came with you. And then I thought, ah, how terrible it would be if we finally owe to the white man not only our destruction, but also our glory. . . . Farewell, Cody. You were my friend. And, indeed, you still are. . . . I never killed you . . . because I *knew it would not matter.*

(*He starts to leave.*)

BUFFALO BILL

If only I could have saved *your* life!

(SITTING BULL *stops and stares at him coldly; turns and leaves. Long pause.*)

BUFFALO BILL

Well! This is it!

(*He forces a weak laugh.*)

Naturally, I've been thinking 'bout this moment for quite some time now. As any performer would.

VOICE

And now to close!

BUFFALO BILL

NOT YET! . . . I would . . . first . . . like to . . . say a few
words in defense of my country's Indian policy, which seems, in
certain circles, to be meeting with considerable disapproval.
(*He smiles weakly, clears his throat, reaches into his pocket,
draws out some notes, and puts on a pair of eyeglasses.*)
The—uh—State of Georgia, anxious to solidify its boundaries
and acquire certain valuable mineral rights, hitherto held ac-
cidentally by the Cherokee Indians, and anxious, furthermore,
to end the seemingly inevitable hostilities between its residents
and these Indians on the question of land ownership, initiated,
last year, the forced removal of the Cherokee nation, resettling
them in a lovely and relatively unsettled area west of the
Mississippi, known as the Mojave Desert. Given proper irriga-
tion, this spacious place should soon be blooming. Reports that
the Cherokees were unhappy at their removal are decidedly
untrue. And though many, naturally, died while marching from
Georgia to the Mojave Desert, the ones who did, I'm told, were
rather ill already, and nothing short of medication could have
saved them. Indeed, in all ways, our vast country is speedily
being opened for settlement. The shipment of smallpox-
infested blankets, sent by the Red Cross to the Mandan Indians, has, I'm pleased to say, worked wonders, and the
Mandans are no more. Also, the Government policy of exter-
minating the buffalo, a policy with which I myself was in-
timately connected, has practically reached fruition. Almost no
buffalo are now left, and soon the Indians will be hungry
enough to begin farming in earnest, a step we believe necessary if they are ever to leave their barbaric ways and enter
civilization. Indeed, it is for this very reason that we have
begun giving rifles to the Indians as part of each treaty with
them, for without armaments they could not hope to wage
war with us, and the process of civilizing them would be
seriously hampered in every way. Another aspect of our
benevolent attitude toward these savages is shown by the
Government's policy of having its official interpreters translate

everything incorrectly when interpreting for the Indians, thereby angering the Indians and forcing them to learn English for themselves. Which, of course, is the first step in civilizing people. I'm reminded here of a story told me by a munitions manufacturer. It seems, by *accident,* he sent a shipment of blank bullets to the Kickapoo Indians, and . . .
(*He looks around.*)
Well, I won't tell it. It's too involved. I would just like to say that I am sick and tired of these sentimental humanitarians who take no account of the difficulties under which this Government has labored in its efforts to deal fairly with the Indian, nor of the countless lives we have lost and atrocities endured at their savage hands. I quote General Sheridan:——
(*The* INDIANS *have begun to rise from their graves; for a while they stand in silence behind* BUFFALO BILL, *where they are joined, at intervals, by the rest of the* INDIAN *company.*)
——"I do not know how far these so-called humanitarians should be excused on account of their political ignorance; but surely it is the only excuse that can give a shadow of justification for their aiding and abetting such horrid crimes as the Indians have perpetrated on our people."

BUFFALO BILL
The excuse that the Indian way of life is vastly different from ours, and that what seem like atrocities to us do not to them, does not hold water, I'm afraid!

SITTING BULL
(*Very softly.*)
I am Sitting Bull——

(*Almost inaudible.*)
——and I am—
dying!

For the truth is, the Indian never had any real title to the soil of this country. We had that title. By *right of discovery!* And all the Indians were, were the *temporary occupants* of the

BLACK HAWK
Black Hawk *is dying.*

TECUMSEH
Tecumseh *is dying.*

land. They *had* to be
vanquished by us! It was,
in fact, our *moral obligation!*

For the earth was given to
mankind to support the
greatest number of which it
is capable; and no tribe or
people have a *right* to
withhold from the wants
of others! For example——

——in the case of Lone Wolf
versus Hitchcock, 1902, the
Supreme Court of the United
States ruled that the power
exists to abrogate the pro-
visions of *any* Indian treaty
if the *interests of the country
demand!*

Here's another one: in the
case of the Seneca Indians
versus the Pennsylvania
Power Authority, the courts
ruled that the Seneca Treaty
was invalid since perpetuity
was legally a vague phrase.
Vague phrase! Yes. Ah.
Here's one, even better.
In the——

No. Wait. Got it. The one
I've been looking for. In
the case of Sitting Bull

CRAZY HORSE
Crazy Horse . . . is dying.

RED CLOUD
Red Cloud *is dying.*

SPOTTED TAIL
Spotted Tail . . . is dying
again.

SATANTA
Satanta *is dying.*

KIOKUK
Kiokuk *is dying.*

GERONIMO
Geronimo . . . *is dying!*

OLD TAZA
Old Taza *is dying!*

JOHN GRASS
John Grass is dying.
(*Long pause.*)

(*The* INDIANS *begin a soft and
mournful moaning.*)

versus Buffalo Bill, the
Supreme Court ruled that the
inadvertent slaughter of . . .
buffalo by . . . I'm sorry,
I'm . . . reminded here of an
amusing story told me by
General Custer. You
remember him—one o' the
great dumbass . . .

(*Pause.*)

BUFFALO BILL

Think I'd better close. I . . . just want to say that anyone
who thinks we have done something wrong is *wrong!* And
that I have here, in this bag, some——
(*He goes and picks up his satchel; he looks up and sees the*
INDIANS *staring at him; he turns quickly away.*)
——Indian trinkets. Some . . . examples of their excellent
workmanship. Moccasins. Beads. Feathered headdresses for
your children.
(*He has begun to unpack these trinkets and place them, for
display, on a small camp stool he has set across the front edge
of the center ring.*)
Pretty picture postcards. Tiny Navaho dolls. The money from
the sale of these few trifling trinkets will go to help them help
themselves. Encourage them a bit. You know, *raise their
spirits.* . . . Ah! Wait. No, sorry, that's a—uh—buffalo skin.
(*He shoves it back in the satchel.*)
Yes. Here it is! Look, just look . . . at this handsome replica
of an . . . Indian. Made of genuine wood.
(*He puts the carved head of an Indian on the camp stool so
that it overlooks all the other trinkets.*

*The lights now slowly begin to fade on him; he sits by the
trinkets, trembling.*)

CHIEF JOSEPH

Tell General Howard I know his heart. I am tired of fighting.
Our chiefs have been killed. Looking Glass is dead. The old

men are all dead. It is cold and we have no blankets. The children are freezing. My people, some of them, have fled to the hills and have no food or warm clothing. No one knows where they are—perhaps frozen. I want to have time to look for my children and see how many of them I can find. Maybe I shall find them among the dead.

(*Almost all the lights are now gone;* CHIEF JOSEPH *can hardly be seen;* BUFFALO BILL *is but a shadow. Only the trinkets are clear in a pinspot of light, and that light, too, is fading.*)

Hear me, my chiefs. I am tired. My heart is sick and sad. From where the sun now stands, I will fight no more, forever.

(*And then, very slowly, even the light on the trinkets fades. And the stage is completely dark.*

Then, suddenly, all lights blazing!

Rodeo ring up.

Rodeo music.

Enter, on horseback, the ROUGHRIDERS OF THE WORLD. *They tour the ring triumphantly, then form a line to greet* BUFFALO BILL, *who enters on his white stallion. He tours the ring, a glassy smile on his face.*

The ROUGHRIDERS *exit.*

BUFFALO BILL *alone, on his horse. He waves his big Stetson to the unseen crowd.*

Then, INDIANS *appear from the shadows outside the ring; they approach him slowly.*

Lights fade to black.

Pause.

Lights return to the way they were at the top of the show, when the audience was entering.

The three glass cases are back in place.

No curtain.)

WINGS

To George Kopit, my father
1913–1977

Preface

In the fall of 1976, I was commissioned to write an original
radio play for Earplay, the drama project of National Public
Radio. They did not stipulate what the play should be about,
only that it should not last longer than an hour. *Wings* was
the result. It has since, of course, been altered and
expanded, mainly to accommodate the visual components of
my central character's condition. But the play was, and still
remains, essentially about language disorder and its
implications. For that reason, radio was the perfect initial
medium; it did not permit me to get lost in the myriad and
always fascinating perceptual aberrations that can
accompany any severe damage to the brain. I now believe
that if I had conceived *Wings* directly for the stage instead, I
would have inevitably found myself seduced by the stage's
greater freedom into investigating at length these astonishing
but ultimately peripheral aspects of aphasia. Most likely,
more characters would have been introduced, a welter of
extraordinary syndromes revealed and examined. If brain
damage is terrifying to behold, it is also alluring. One feels
the need to avert one's eyes and hide, and the equal if not
greater need to keep looking. It is a very scary business, this
job of exploring who we are. Very quickly, I suspect, my
focus would have vanished. All of which is to say that if
Wings exhibits in its present form any excellence of vision
and craft, that excellence is without question a direct function
of the rigor imposed on it by its initial incarnation. For that
reason, I must express a deep debt of gratitude to Earplay
for having commissioned this play, and particularly to the
man who directed both its initial version and its first
production on the stage at Yale, John Madden.

There is a question which I suspect must arise inevitably in
the mind of anyone who reads or sees this play: to what
degree is *Wings* faithful to fact, to what degree sheer
speculation.

In the spring of 1976, seven months before Earplay was to
commission me to write on a subject of my choosing, my
father suffered a major stroke which rendered him incapable
of speech. Furthermore, because of certain other

complications, all related to his aphasia, and all typical of
stroke, it was impossible to know how much he
comprehended. Certainly there was no doubt that his
capacity to comprehend had been drastically impaired and
reduced. As best I could, I tried to understand what he was
going through. It seemed to me that, regardless of how
reduced his senses were, the isolation he was being forced
to endure had to verge on the intolerable; clearly, he had not
lost all comprehension—the look of terror in his eyes was
unmistakable. Yet, not only did he tolerate this state; every
now and then, if one watched carefully enough, something
escaped from this shell that was his body and his prison,
something almost but not quite palpable, something not
readily brought to the attention of a nurse (I tried it once but
she saw nothing), something which I felt possessed a kind of
glow or flicker, rather like a lamp way off in the dark,
something only barely perceptible. I took these faint flashes
to be him signaling. And although I allowed for the possibility
that what I was perceiving was nothing but mirage, or the
mirrored reflections of my own hopeful and constant
signalings to him, nonetheless, it seemed to me (indeed,
seemed irrefutable) that in some ineffably essential way,
reduced as he was, he was still the same person he had
been. This thought was both heartening and frightful. To
what extent was he still intact? To what extent was he aware
of what had befallen him? *What was it like inside?*

And then Earplay came along. By its very nature, radio
seemed to offer an especially appropriate means of exploring
these particular questions.

I recognized at once that I could not deal directly with my
father. For one thing, I was too close to him to hold any
hope of objectivity. For another, his case was too severe, too
grim, my audience would turn away. So I looked elsewhere
for a model. The questions would remain the same, of
course, and just as valid; my understanding of my father's
world would have to come—if indeed it could at all—through
analogy. I decided to focus on two patients I had met at the
Burke Rehabilitation Center in White Plains, New York, where

my father had been transferred after his stay in the hospital. Both were women: one was old, in her late seventies, perhaps older; the other, not quite thirty. Like my father, both had suffered major strokes, though neither was as incapacitated as he; both at least could talk. Certainly they could not talk well.

The speech of the younger woman was fluent and possessed normal intonations, cadence, and syntactical structure—in fact, to such an extent that anyone who did not understand English would have sworn she was making sense. Nonetheless, her sentences were laced with a kind of babbled jargon so that, by and large, she made no sense at all. In her early stages, she seemed unaware of this appalling deficit.* In contrast, the older woman's words had no fluency, no melodic inflection, no syntactical richness. Her words emerged with difficulty and sounded like something composed for a telegram. Modifiers and conjunctions for the most part were absent. But at least her words made sense. The problem was, as often as not, the sense they conveyed was not the sense she intended. Though she usually was aware of these "mistakes," or at least could be made aware of them, she could not prevent them from occurring. Neither could she readily correct them. Aside from her aphasia, each woman was relatively free of other symptoms.

I had met the older woman while accompanying my father one afternoon on his rounds. When he went down for speech therapy, she was one of the three other patients in the room. I had never observed a speech therapy session before and was nervous. The day, I recall vividly, was warm, humid. The windows of the room were open. A scent of flowers suffused the air. To get the session started, the therapist asked the older woman if she could name the seasons of the year. With much effort, she did, though not in

*This particular kind of speech, typical of a certain form of aphasia, is characterized by neologisms, and sounds very much like double talk or gibberish. The word *gibberish,* however, suggests psychosis and dementia, and is therefore inappropriate for describing an effect of organic brain disease; the term *jargonaphasia* is used instead.

proper order. She seemed annoyed with herself for having
any difficulty at all with such a task. The therapist then asked
her which of these seasons corresponded to the present.
The woman turned at once to the window. She could see the
garden, the flowers. Her eyes were clear, alert; there was no
question but that she understood what was wanted. I cannot
remember having ever witnessed such an intense struggle.
At first, she did nothing but sit calmly and wait for the word
to arrive on its own. When it didn't, she tried to force the
word out by herself, through thinking; as if to assist what
clearly was a process of expulsion, she scrunched her face
up, squeezed her eyelids shut. But no word emerged.
Physically drained, her face drenched with sweat, she tried
another trick: she cocked her head and listened to the birds,
whose sound was incessant. When this too led to nothing,
she sniffed the air. When nothing came of this strategy
either, she turned her attention to what she was wearing, a
light cotton dress; she even touched the fabric. Finally,
something connected. Her lips began to form a word. She
shut her eyes. Waited. The word emerged. *Winter.*

When informed that it was summer she seemed astonished,
how was it possible? . . . a mistake like that . . . obviously
she knew what season it was, anyone with eyes could tell at
once what season it was! . . . and yet . . . She looked over
at where I sat and shook her head in dismay, then laughed
and said, "This is really nuts, isn't it!"

I sat there, stunned. I could not believe that anyone making
a mistake of such gross proportions and with such
catastrophic implications could laugh at it.

So there would be no misunderstanding, the therapist quickly
pointed out that this mistake stemmed completely from her
stroke; in no way was she demented. The woman smiled
(she knew all that) and turned away, stared back out the
window at the garden. *This is really nuts, isn't it!*—I could not
get her phrase from my mind. In its intonation, it had
conveyed no feeling of anger, resignation, or despair. Rather,
it had conveyed amazement, and in that amazement, a trace

(incredible as it seemed) of delight. This is not to suggest that anyone witnessing this incident could, even for an instant, have imagined that she was in any sense pleased with her condition. The amazement, and its concomitant delight, seemed to me to reflect only an acknowledgment that her condition was extraordinary, and in no way denied or obviated the terror or the horror that were at its core. By some (I supposed) nourishing spring of inner strength and light, of whose source I had no idea, she had come to a station in her life from which she could perceive in what was happening something that bore the aspect of adventure, and it was through this perhaps innate capacity to perceive and appreciate adventure, and perhaps in this sense only, that she found some remaining modicum of delight, which I suspect kept her going. Of course, all this was speculation. As I said, I was stunned. The therapist asked her to try again and she did. And she got it—summer! With great excitement, she tried once again. Same result. She had it! Summer! She tried again. *Winter.* It was lost. She heard but could do nothing. She shook her head in consternation. Smiled in wonderment. In the course of the session, I discovered we shared the same birthday.

Later that afternoon, I inquired as to who she was, and was told she was a former aviatrix and wing-walker. I believe my response to this news was *"What?"*—although I think I may have said, *"Wing-walker?"* Either way, my composure was slipping. I felt decidedly inadequate.

A nurse brought me to her room (she was out, gone down to dinner) and showed me a photograph pinned up on her wall; it had been taken when she was in her twenties. In the photograph, a biplane sits on a large grassy field, a crowded grandstand in the distance, its front railing draped with flags. The plane is a Curtiss Jenny. A pilot sits in the rearmost of its two open cockpits; she is standing out on its lower wing, white silk scarf around her neck, goggles set back on top of her leather helmet. She wears jodhpurs, boots, a leather jacket. Her face is lean and handsome and imperious. The same noble and slightly quizzical smile I'd seen that afternoon is there. Her right hand is holding on to the wire stays behind her. The propeller is spinning; apparently, her plane is about to take off. Several nurses come in and join us in staring at the photograph. Her eyes seem on fire; they are filled with an unquenchable eager passion. Her left hand is waving toward the camera and the unseen throng.

Needless to say, had I invented her, the invention would have been excessive, would have strained credulity—only in dreams and fiction did one meet persons such as this. Yet, here she was, she existed. Everyone at Burke who knew her agreed that the fortitude and *esprit* I'd seen that afternoon in the therapy session were no aberration. By nature she was one of the bravest, most extraordinary persons they had ever met. There was no other choice: she was my model.

With that decision, a task that might otherwise have been little more than grim took on the aspects of an adventure. As scrupulously as possible, I would try to explore, through her mind, this terrible and awesome realm of being. Surely, that realm bore resemblance to my father's. Courage was not her quality alone.

The title came at once. Also, with it, two recognitions: if *Wings* was to be effective, it would have to deal specifically with its central character and not with some general condition called stroke; at the same time, to be effective, it would have to possess an absolutely solid clinical accuracy.

To these ends, I began an exhaustive study of airplanes and brain damage—unquestionably a weird conjunction of subjects. The study of airplanes was simple. Libraries provided everything I had to know about early aviation—how the old biplanes were flown, who flew them, what their cockpits looked like, felt like; and especially about that remarkable post-World War I phenomenon known as barnstorming, when pilots (many of them women) toured the country, thrilling crowds with exhibitions of their marvelous, death-defying daring and skill. Burke was where I went to study brain damage and rehabilitation.

It quickly became clear that, for my purposes at least, the speech patterns of this older woman (due to the nature of her stroke) were not as varied and therefore not as interesting as the speech patterns of many other patients.

For greater linguistic richness, I turned to the patient in her late twenties as the principal model for my central character's speech. In her own right, this young woman was as exceptional as the older. Certainly she was no less brave. When I met her, she was able to acknowledge the gravity of her condition, and fought all tendencies to self-pity and despair. With as much cheerfulness as she could muster (her capacity for hope seemed limitless), she worked every moment that she could at the one task in her life that mattered: the reassembling of her shattered world. But there was yet another exceptional aspect to this young woman, and in truth it was this that made me turn to her as the model not only for my central character's patterns of speech but, in fact, ultimately, her very processes of thought: *she was left-handed.* From this one seemingly insignificant trait, many remarkable abilities derived.

In a right-handed person, the left hemisphere of the cerebral cortex is dominant and controls all activities connected with speech and analytic consciousness. However, for persons who are by nature left-handed, some of the left hemisphere's usual functions are taken over by the normally nonverbal and intuitive right. Should such a person suffer a stroke or injury to the left cerebral hemisphere, he stands a good chance of retaining a degree of verbal lucidity and insight inaccessible to those whose left hemisphere maintains sole dominance. This was the case with the young woman I met at Burke. Because of her left-handedness, she possessed the rare ability to recognize and articulate, to a slight but still significant extent, her own patterns of thought. Repeatedly, she would describe a certain dividedness within her head, as if she literally sensed the separate hemispheres at work, usually in contradiction to each other. In such instances, she would actually refer to her mind's "two sides," and frequently accompany this description with a slicing gesture of her hand, clearly suggestive of a vertically symmetrical division of her entire body. Once, she described coming to a large puddle. With great amusement she recounted how one side of her head told her to go left, while the other side told her to go right; to end the controversy and resolve the debate, she walked through the middle.

At Burke I studied her attempts at keeping a journal, listened to hours of taped interviews between her and her speech therapist, and of course, as often as possible, talked directly to her myself. She seemed to understand something of my project and its purposes, and seemed pleased that somehow she could be of help. Gradually, an image of a remarkable and quite vivid interior landscape began to form in my mind, frightening and awesome in its details, its blatant gaps, its implications.

But there was still another person crucial to my research: her therapist, Jacqueline Doolittle. Her knowledge of aphasia was my touchstone. At all hours of the day and sometimes night, I would call Mrs. Doolittle with some generally naïve question about the brain, and she, with limitless good humor, would set me straight. It is both astonishing and humbling the number of assumptions one can make in this field which are absolutely wrong. Nonetheless, I kept phoning and, if not phoning, stopping by her office, usually unannounced. To her credit, and perhaps to mine, she never threw me out. Gradually, things became clearer. I should point out, Mrs. Doolittle's understanding of aphasia went far beyond the clinical: Jacqueline Doolittle had herself been aphasic once.

Her aphasia had resulted from a head injury sustained in an auto accident. Eventually she recovered, and her recollections of this period are like visions of a sojourn in another realm: vivid and detailed. Without a doubt, it was this experience that lay at the root of her exceptional empathic abilities as a therapist.

What she described was a world of fragments, a world without dimension, a world where time meant nothing constant, and from which there seemed no method of escape. She thought she had either gone mad or been captured by an unknown enemy for purposes she could not fathom, and in fact took the hospital she was in to be a farmhouse in disguise, controlled by her captors. For a long time, she was unable to distinguish that the words she spoke were jargon, and wondered why everyone she saw spoke to her in a foreign tongue. Her state was one of utter isolation, confusion, terror, and disarray. She wondered if perhaps she was dreaming. Sometimes the thought occurred to her that she was dead. Then, very gradually, the swelling in her head subsided, and little by little the cells in her left cerebral hemisphere began to make their proper neural connections. She began to understand what people said. When she spoke, the right words, as if by magic, started flowing. She returned to the world she knew. *Wings* owes much of its structure and detail to these recollections.

How much of this play, then, is speculation?

Wings is a play about a woman whom I have called Emily Stilson. Though she suffers a stroke, in no way is it a case study, and in its execution I have assiduously avoided any kind of clinical or documentary approach. Indeed, it has been so conceived and constructed that its audience can, for the most part, observe this realm that she is in only through her own consciousness. In short, *Wings* is a work of speculation informed by fact.

But any attempt to render a person's consciousness through words, even autobiography, must be speculative. Where thoughts are concerned, there are no infallible reporters. What we remember of our pasts is filtered by our sensibilities and predilections, and can as easily be imaginary as real. To what extent did Jacqui Doolittle remember only what she wanted to? To what extent did her mind, in its damaged state, withhold from her consciousness something essential to her experience? Given that she was suffering a severe language deficit, how much can we trust her verbal recollections? In this arena, hard facts do not exist. Yet, if we cannot hope for what is provable, we at least can strive for what is plausible. By any criteria, Jacqui Doolittle's account has emotional validity. The same holds true for the young left-handed woman's. It was this emotional truth, informed by fact, that I was after. So far as I was able, I have avoided in this play any colorations of my own and, as far as I know, have attributed to Emily Stilson no symptoms that are unlikely or impossible. Though Emily Stilson is a composite of many persons, and derives finally from my imagination, I have worked as if in fact she existed, and in this light, and within the limitations of this form, have felt myself obliged to render her condition as it was, not as I might have preferred it.

There are two books whose influence on me I would like to acknowledge, and which I strongly recommend to anyone interested in further explorations of this subject: Howard Gardner's *The Shattered Mind,* and A. R. Luria's *The Man with a Shattered World.*

I would also like to acknowledge the crucial role of Robert Brustein, as Dean of the Yale School of Drama, in the evolution of this play. Mr. Brustein had heard the radio play performed, and had expressed his admiration of the work. In November of 1977, he called me to say that he had been thinking about the play, and had come to believe it could be even more effective on the stage. A slot had opened in the Yale Rep's spring schedule. Was I interested?

Not only was I interested, I was flabbergasted. Since summer, when I had first heard *Wings* performed, I had been trying to figure out if it was possible to adapt it to the stage. The problems, it turned out, were considerable, both structurally and thematically. That afternoon, indeed less than an hour before the call came in, I had suddenly realized how to do it.

For those who may have missed the issue, *Forbes Magazine* ranks playwrighting extremely low on the list of Easy Ways to

Earn One's Fortune. In fact, it is no simple matter to earn one's living at its practice. I would therefore like to express both my family's and my deep gratitude to the Rockefeller Foundation for a generous and timely grant, which alone enabled me to devote, with ease of mind, the enormous time and energy that I soon found the work demanded, both in the writing and in the research.

For their extensive and always generous assistance in that research, I am profoundly indebted and grateful to the Burke Rehabilitation Center; and especially to Jacqueline Doolittle.

A.L.K.

Wings opened at the Lyceum Theatre, New York on January 28, 1979, with the following cast:

Characters

Emily Stilson   Constance Cummings
Amy   Mary-Joan Negro
Doctors   Roy Steinberg
              Ross Petty
Nurses   Gina Franz
             Mary Michelle Rutherford
Billy   James Tolkan
Mr. Brownstein   Carl Don
Mrs. Timmins   Betty Pelzer

Directed by   John Madden
Designed by   Andrew Jackness
Costumes by   Jeanne Button
Lighting by   Tom Schraeder
Sound by   Tom Voegeli
Music by   Herb Pilhofer

The play takes place over a period of two years; it should be performed without an intermission.

I weave in and out of the strange clouds, hidden in my tiny cockpit, submerged, alone, on the magnitude of this weird, unhuman space, venturing where man has never been, perhaps never meant to go. Am I myself a living, breathing, earth-bound body, or is this a dream of death I'm passing through? Am I alive, or am I really dead, a spirit in a spirit world. Am I actually in a plane, or have I crashed on some worldly mountain, and is this the afterlife?

Charles Lindbergh, *The Spirit of St. Louis*.

Notes on the production of this play

The stage as a void

System of black scrim panels that can move silently and easily, creating the impression of featureless, labyrinthine corridors.

Some panels mirrored so they can fracture light, create the impression of endlessness, even airiness, multiply and confound images, confound one's sense of space.

Sound both live and pre-recorded, amplified; speakers all around the theater.

No attempt should be made to create a literal representation of Mrs. Stilson's world, especially since Mrs. Stilson's world is no longer in any way literal.

The scenes should blend. No clear boundaries or domains in time or space for Mrs. Stilson any more.

It is posited by this play that the woman we see in the center of the void is the intact inner self of Mrs. Stilson. This inner self does not need to move physically when her external body (which we cannot see) moves. Thus, we infer movement from the context; from whatever clues we can obtain. It is the same for her, of course. She learns as best she can.

And yet, sometimes, the conditions change; then the woman we observe is Mrs. Stilson as others see her. We thus infer who it is we are seeing from the context, too. Sometimes we see both the inner and outer self at once.

Nothing about her world is predictable or consistent. This fact is its essence.

The progression of the play is from fragmentation to integration. By the end, boundaries have become somewhat clearer. But she remains always in another realm from us.

Prelude

AS AUDIENCE ENTERS, A COZY ARMCHAIR VISIBLE
DOWNSTAGE IN A POOL OF LIGHT, DARKNESS
SURROUNDING IT.

A CLOCK HEARD TICKING IN THE DARK.

LIGHTS TO BLACK.

HOLD.

WHEN THE LIGHTS COME BACK, EMILY STILSON, A
WOMAN WELL INTO HER SEVENTIES, IS SITTING IN THE
ARMCHAIR READING A BOOK. SOME DISTANCE AWAY, A
FLOOR LAMP GLOWS DIMLY. ON THE OTHER SIDE OF
HER CHAIR, ALSO SOME DISTANCE AWAY, A SMALL
TABLE WITH A CLOCK. THE CHAIR, THE LAMP, AND THE
TABLE WITH THE CLOCK ALL SIT ISOLATED IN NARROW
POOLS OF LIGHT, DARKNESS BETWEEN AND AROUND
THEM.

THE CLOCK SEEMS TO BE TICKING A TRIFLE LOUDER
THAN NORMAL.

MRS. STILSON, ENJOYING HER BOOK AND THE
PLEASANT EVENING, READS ON SERENELY.

AND THEN SHE LOOKS UP.

THE LAMP DISAPPEARS INTO THE DARKNESS.

BUT SHE TURNS BACK TO HER BOOK AS IF NOTHING
ODD HAS HAPPENED; RESUMES READING.

AND THEN, A MOMENT LATER, SHE LOOKS UP AGAIN,
AN EXPRESSION OF SLIGHT PERPLEXITY ON HER FACE.
FOR NO DISCERNIBLE REASON, SHE TURNS TOWARD
THE CLOCK.

THE CLOCK AND THE TABLE IT IS SITTING ON
DISAPPEAR INTO THE DARKNESS.

SHE TURNS FRONT. STARES OUT INTO SPACE.

THEN SHE TURNS BACK TO HER BOOK. RESUMES
READING. BUT THE READING SEEMS AN EFFORT; HER
MIND IS ON OTHER THINGS.

THE CLOCK SKIPS A BEAT.

ONLY AFTER THE CLOCK HAS RESUMED ITS NORMAL
RHYTHM DOES SHE LOOK UP. IT IS AS IF THE SKIPPED
BEAT HAS ONLY JUST THEN REGISTERED. FOR THE
FIRST TIME, SHE DISPLAYS WHAT ONE MIGHT CALL
CONCERN.

AND THEN THE CLOCK STOPS AGAIN. THIS TIME THE
INTERVAL LASTS LONGER.

THE BOOK SLIPS OUT OF MRS. STILSON'S HANDS; SHE
STARES OUT IN TERROR.

BLACKOUT.

NOISE.

The moment of a stroke, even a relatively minor one, and its immediate aftermath, are an experience in chaos. Nothing at all makes sense. Nothing except perhaps this overwhelming disorientation will be remembered by the victim. The stroke usually happens suddenly. It is a catastrophe.

It is my intention that the audience recognize that some real event is occurring; that real information is being received by the victim, but that it is coming in too scrambled and too fast to be properly decoded. Systems overload.

And so this section must not seem like utter "noise," though certainly it must be more noisy than intelligible. I do not believe there is any way to be true to this material if it is not finally "composed" in rehearsal, on stage, by "feel." Theoretically, any sound or image herein described can occur anywhere in this section. The victim cannot process. Her familiar world has been rearranged. The puzzle is in pieces. All at once, and with no time to prepare, she has been picked up and dropped into another realm.

In order that this section may be put together in rehearsal (there being no one true "final order" to the images and sounds she perceives), I have divided this section into three discrete parts with the understanding that in performance these parts will blend together to form one cohesive whole.

The first group consists of the visual images Mrs. Stilson perceives.

The second group consists of those sounds emanating outside herself. Since these sounds are all filtered by her mind, and since her mind has been drastically altered, the question of whether we in the audience are hearing what is actually occurring or only hearing what she believes is occurring is unanswerable.

The third group contains Mrs. Stilson's words: the words she thinks and the words she speaks. Since we are perceiving the world through Mrs. Stilson's senses, there is no sure way

for us to know whether she is actually saying any of these
words aloud.

Since the experience we are exploring is not one of logic but
its opposite, there is no logical reason for these groupings to
occur in the order in which I have presented them. These are
but components, building blocks, and can therefore be
repeated, spliced, reversed, filtered, speeded up or slowed
down. What should determine their final sequence and
juxtaposition, tempi, intensity, is the "musical" sense of this
section as a whole; it must pulse and build. An explosion
quite literally is occurring in her brain, or rather, a series of
explosions: the victim's mind, her sense of time and place,
her sense of self, all are being shattered if not annihilated.
Fortunately, finally, she will pass out. Were her head a
pinball game it would register TILT—game over—stop.
Silence. And resume again. Only now the victim is in yet
another realm. The Catastrophe section is the journey or the
fall into this strange and dreadful realm.

In the world into which Mrs. Stilson has been so violently
and suddenly transposed, time and place are without
definition. The distance from her old familiar world is
immense. For all she knows, she could as well be on
another planet.

In this new world, she moves from one space or thought or
concept to another without willing or sometimes even
knowing it. Indeed, when she moves in this maze-like place,
it is as if the world around her and not she were doing all the
moving. To her, there is nothing any more that is
commonplace or predictable. Nothing is as it was. Everything
comes as a surprise. Something has relieved her of
command. Something beyond her comprehension has her in
its grip.

In the staging of this play, the sense should therefore be
conveyed of physical and emotional separation (by the use,
for example, of the dark transparent screens through which
her surrounding world can be only dimly and partly seen, or

by alteration of external sound) and of total immersion in strangeness.

Because our focus is on Mrs. Stilson's inner self, it is important that she exhibit no particular overt physical disabilities. Furthermore, we should never see her in a wheelchair, even though, were we able to observe her through the doctors' eyes, a wheelchair is probably what she would, more often than not, be in.

One further note: because Mrs. Stilson now processes information at a different rate from us, there is no reason that what we see going on around her has to be the visual equivalent of what we hear.

Catastrophe

Images	Sounds outside herself
	(SOUNDS live or on tape, altered or unadorned)
	Of wind.
Mostly, it is whiteness. Dazzling, blinding.	Of someone breathing with effort, unevenly.
	Of something ripping, like a sheet.
Occasionally, there are brief rhombs of color, explosions of color, the color red being dominant.	Of something flapping, the sound suggestive of an old screen door perhaps, or a sheet or sail in the wind. It is a rapid fibrilation. And it is used mostly to mark transitions. It can seem ominous or not.
The mirrors, of course, reflect infinitely. Sense of endless space, endless corridors.	Of a woman's scream (though this sound should be altered by filters so it resembles other things, such as sirens).
	Of random noises recorded in a busy city hospital, then altered so as to be only minimally recognizable.
Nothing seen that is not a fragment. Every aspect of her world has been shattered.	Of a car's engine at full speed.
	Of a siren (altered to resemble a woman screaming).
Utter isolation.	Of an airplane coming closer, thundering overhead, then zooming off into silence.

Mrs. Stilson's voice

(VOICE live or on tape,
altered or unadorned)

*Oh my God oh my God oh
my God—*

*—trees clouds houses
mostly planes flashing past,
images without words, utter
disarray disbelief, never seen
this kind of thing before!*

*Where am I? How'd I get
here?*

*My leg (What's my leg?)
feels wet arms . . . wet too,
belly same chin nose
everything (Where are they
taking me?) something sticky
(What has happened to my
plane?) feel something
sticky.*

Doors! Too many doors!

*Must have . . . fallen cannot
. . . move at all sky . . .
(Gliding!) dark cannot . . .
talk (Feel as if I'm gliding!).*

*Yes, feels cool, nice . . .
Yes, this is the life all right!*

Images	Sounds outside herself

In this vast whiteness, like apparitions, partial glimpses of doctors and nurses can be seen. They appear and disappear like a pulse. They are never in one place for long. The mirrors multiply their incomprehensibility.

Of random crowd noises, the crowd greatly agitated. In the crowd, people can be heard calling for help, a doctor, an ambulance. But all the sounds are garbled.

Of people whispering.

Of many people asking questions simultaneously, no question comprehensible.

Sometimes the dark panels are opaque, sometimes transparent. Always, they convey a sense of layers, multiplicity, separation. Sense constantly of doors opening, closing, opening, closing.

Of doors opening, closing, opening, closing.

Of someone breathing oxygen through a mask.

VOICES (garbled): Just relax. / No one's going to hurt you. / Can you hear us? / Be careful! / You're hurting her! / No, we're not. / Don't lift her, leave her where she is! / Someone call an ambulance! / I don't think she can hear.

Fragments of hospital equipment appear out of nowhere and disappear just as suddenly. Glimpse always too brief to enable us to identify what this equipment is, or what its purpose.

MALE VOICE: Have you any idea—

OTHER VOICES (garbled): Do you know your name? / Do you know where you are? / What year is this? / If I say the tiger has been killed by the lion, which animal is dead?

Mrs. Stilson's movements seem random. She is a person wandering through space, lost.

A hospital paging system heard.

Mrs. Stilson's voice

*My plane! What has
happened to my plane!*

Help . . .

*—all around faces of which
nothing known no sense
ever all wiped out blank like
ice I think saw it once flying
over something some place
all was white sky and sea
clouds ice almost crashed
couldn't tell where I was
heading right side up
topsy-turvy under over I was
flying actually if I can I do
yes do recall was upside
down can you believe it
almost scraped my head on
the ice caps couldn't tell
which way was up wasn't
even dizzy strange things
happen to me that they do!*

*What's my name? I don't
know my name!*

*Where's my arm? I don't
have an arm!*

What's an arm?

Images	Sounds outside herself
Finally, Mrs. Stilson is led by attendants downstage, to a chair. Then left alone.	Equipment being moved through stone corridors, vast vaulting space. Endless echoing.

Mrs. Stilson's voice

*AB-ABC-ABC123DE451212
what? 123—12345678972357
better yes no problem I'm
okay soon be out soon be
over storm . . . will pass I'm
sure. Always has.*

Awakening

In performance, the end of the Catastrophe section should blend, without interruption, into the beginning of this.

MRS. STILSON DOWNSTAGE ON A CHAIR IN A POOL OF
LIGHT, DARKNESS ALL AROUND HER. IN THE DISTANCE
BEHIND HER, MUFFLED SOUNDS OF A HOSPITAL.
VAGUE IMAGES OF DOCTORS, NURSES ATTENDING TO
SOMEONE WE CANNOT SEE. ONE OF THE DOCTORS
CALLS MRS. STILSON'S NAME. DOWNSTAGE, MRS.
STILSON SHOWS NO TRACE OF RECOGNITION. THE
DOCTOR CALLS HER NAME AGAIN. AGAIN NO
RESPONSE. ONE OF THE DOCTORS SAYS, "IT'S
POSSIBLE SHE MAY HEAR US BUT BE UNABLE TO
RESPOND."

ONE OF THE NURSES TRIES CALLING OUT HER NAME.
STILL NO RESPONSE. THE DOCTOR LEAVES. THE
REMAINING DOCTORS AND NURSES FADE INTO THE
DARKNESS.

ONLY MRS. STILSON CAN BE SEEN.

PAUSE.

MRS. STILSON: *Still . . . sun moon too or . . . three times
happened maybe globbidged rubbidged uff and firded-forded
me to nothing there try again* [WE HEAR A WINDOW BEING
RAISED SOMEWHERE BEHIND HER] *window! up and heard*
[SOUNDS OF BIRDS] *known them know I know them once
upon a birds! that's it better getting better soon be out of
this.*

PAUSE.

Out of . . . what?

PAUSE.

*Dark . . . space vast of . . . in I am or so it seems feels no
real clues to speak of.* [BEHIND HER, BRIEF IMAGE OF A
DOCTOR PASSING] *Something tells me I am not alone.
Once! Lost it. No here back thanks work fast now, yes empty
vast reach of space desert think they call it I'll come back to*

that anyhow down I . . . something what [BRIEF IMAGE OF A NURSE] *it's SOMETHING ELSE IS ENTERING MY!—no wait got it crashing OH MY GOD! CRASHING! deadstick dead-of-night thought the stars were airport lights upside down was I what a way to land glad no one there to see it, anyhow tubbish blaxed and vinkled I commenshed to uh-oh where's it gone to somewhere flubbished what?* with [BRIEF IMAGES OF HOSPITAL STAFF ON THE MOVE] *images are SOMETHING ODD IS! . . . yes, then there I thank you crawling sands and knees still can feel it hear the wind all alone somehow wasn't scared why a mystery, vast dark track of space, we've all got to die that I know, anyhow then day came light came with it so with this you'd think you'd hope just hold on they will find me I am . . . still intact.*

PAUSE.

In here.

LONG SILENCE.

Seem to be the word removed.

LONG SILENCE.

How long have I been here? . . . And wrapped in dark.

PAUSE.

Can remember nothing.

OUTSIDE SOUNDS BEGIN TO IMPINGE; SAME FOR IMAGES. IN THE DISTANCE, AN ATTENDANT DIMLY SEEN PUSHING A FLOOR POLISHER. ITS NOISE RESEMBLES AN ANIMAL'S GROWL.

[TRYING HARD TO BE CHEERY]: *No, definitely I am not alone!*

THE SOUND OF THE POLISHER GROWS LOUDER,

SEEMS MORE BESTIAL, VORACIOUS; IT OVERWHELMS
EVERYTHING. EXPLOSION! SHE GASPS.

[RAPIDLY AND IN PANIC, SENSE OF GREAT COMMOTION
BEHIND HER. A CRISIS HAS OCCURRED] *There I go there
I go hallway now it's screaming crowded pokes me then the
coolbreeze needle scent of sweetness can see palms
flowers flummers couldn't fix the leaking sprouting
everywhere to save me help me CUTS UP THROUGH to
something movement I am something moving without
movement!*

SOUND OF A WOMAN'S MUFFLED SCREAM FROM
BEHIND HER. THE SCREAM GROWS LOUDER.

[WITH DELIGHT] *What a strange adventure I am having!*

LIGHTS TO BLACK ON EVERYTHING.

IN THE DARK, A PAUSE.

WHEN HER VOICE IS HEARD AGAIN, IT IS HEARD FIRST
FROM ALL THE SPEAKERS. HER VOICE SOUNDS
GROGGY, SLURRED. NO LONGER ANY SENSE OF PANIC
DISCERNIBLE. A FEW MOMENTS AFTER HER VOICE IS
HEARD, THE LIGHTS COME UP SLOWLY ON HER. SOON,
ONLY SHE IS SPEAKING; THE VOICE FROM THE
SPEAKERS HAS DISAPPEARED.

*Hapst aporkshop fleetish yes of course it's yes the good ol'
times when we would mollis I mean collis all around still what
my son's name is cannot for the life of me yet face gleams
smiles as he tells them what I did but what his name is
cannot see it pleasant anyway yes palms now ocean sea
breeze wafting floating up and lifting holding weightless and
goes swoooping down with me least I . . . think it's me.*

SOUND OF SOMETHING FLAPPING RAPIDLY OPEN AND
CLOSED, OPEN AND CLOSED.

SOUND OF WIND.

LIGHTS CHANGE INTO A COOL AND AIRY BLUE. SENSE
OF WEIGHTLESSNESS, SERENITY.

IN ANOTHER REALM NOW.

*Yes, out there walking not holding even danger ever-present
how I loved it love it still no doubt will again hear them
cheering wisht or waltz away to some place like Rumania . . .*

THE WIND DISAPPEARS.

Nothing . . .

THE SERENE BLUE LIGHT BEGINS TO FADE AWAY.
SOME PLACE ELSE NOW THAT SHE IS GOING.

*Of course beyond that yet 1, 2 came before the yeast rose
bubbled and MY CHUTE DIDN'T OPEN PROPERLY! Still for
a girl did wonders getting down and it was Charles! no
Charlie, who is Charlie? see him smiling as they tell him
what I—*

OUTSIDE WORLD BEGINS TO IMPINGE. LIGHTS ARE
CHANGING, GROWING BRIGHTER, SOMETHING ODD IS
HAPPENING. SENSE OF IMMINENCE. SHE NOTICES.

[BREATHLESS WITH EXCITEMENT]: *Stop hold cut stop wait
stop come-out-break-out light can see it ready heart can yes
can feel it pounding something underway here light is getting
brighter lids I think the word is that's it lifting of their own but
slowly knew I should be patient should be what? wait hold on
steady now it's spreading no no question something
underway here spreading brighter rising lifting light almost
yes can almost there a little more now yes can almost see
this . . . place I'm . . . in and . . .*

LOOK OF HORROR.

Oh my God! Now I understand! THEY'VE GOT ME!

FOR FIRST TIME DOCTORS, NURSES, HOSPITAL
EQUIPMENT ALL CLEARLY VISIBLE BEHIND HER. ALL
ARE GATHERED AROUND SOMEONE WE CANNOT SEE.
FROM THE WAY THEY ARE ALL BENDING OVER, WE
SURMISE THIS PERSON WE CANNOT SEE IS LYING IN A
BED.

LIGHTS DROP ON MRS. STILSON, DOWNSTAGE.

NURSE [TALKING TO THE PERSON UPSTAGE WE
CANNOT SEE]: Mrs. Stilson, can you open up your eyes?

PAUSE.

MRS. STILSON [SEPARATED FROM HER QUESTIONERS
BY GREAT DISTANCE]: *Don't know how.*

DOCTOR: Mrs. Stilson, you just opened up your eyes. We
saw you. Can you open them again?

NO RESPONSE.

Mrs. Stilson . . .?

MRS. STILSON [PROUDLY, TRIUMPHANTLY]: *My name
then—Mrs. Stilson!*

VOICE ON P.A. SYSTEM: Mrs. Howard, call on three! Mrs.
Howard . . . !

MRS. STILSON: *My name then—Mrs. Howard?*

LIGHTS FADE TO BLACK ON HOSPITAL STAFF.

SOUND OF WIND, SENSE OF TIME PASSING.

LIGHTS COME UP ON MRS. STILSON. THE WIND
DISAPPEARS.

The room that I am in is large, square. What does large mean?

PAUSE.

The way I'm turned I can see a window. When I'm on my back the window isn't there.

DOCTOR [IN THE DISTANCE, AT BEST ONLY DIMLY SEEN]: Mrs. Stilson, can you hear me?

MRS. STILSON: *Yes.*

SECOND DOCTOR: Mrs. Stilson, can you hear me?

MRS. STILSON: *Yes! I said yes! What's wrong with you?*

FIRST DOCTOR: Mrs. Stilson, CAN YOU HEAR ME!

MRS. STILSON: *Don't believe this—I've been put in with the deaf!*

SECOND DOCTOR: Mrs. Stilson, if you can hear us, nod your head.

MRS. STILSON: *All right, fine, that's how you want to play it —there!*

SHE NODS.

THE DOCTORS EXCHANGE GLANCES.

FIRST DOCTOR: Mrs. Stilson, if you can hear us, NOD YOUR HEAD!

MRS. STILSON: *Oh my God, this is grotesque!*

CACOPHONY OF SOUNDS HEARD FROM ALL AROUND, BOTH LIVE AND FROM THE SPEAKERS. IMAGES SUGGESTING SENSATION OF ASSAULT AS WELL.

IMPLICATION OF ALL THESE SOUNDS AND IMAGES IS
THAT MRS. STILSON IS BEING MOVED THROUGH THE
HOSPITAL FOR PURPOSES OF EXAMINATION, PERHAPS
EVEN TORTURE. THE INFORMATION WE RECEIVE
COMES IN TOO FAST AND DISTORTED FOR RATIONAL
COMPREHENSION. THE REALM SHE IS IN IS
TERRIFYING. FORTUNATELY, SHE IS NOT IN IT LONG.

AS LONG AS SHE IS, HOWEVER, THE SENSE SHOULD
BE CONVEYED THAT HER WORLD MOVES AROUND HER
MORE THAN SHE THROUGH IT.

WHAT WE HEAR (THE COMPONENTS): Are we moving you
too fast? / Mustlian pottid or blastigrate, no not that way
this, that's fletchit gottit careful now. / Now put your nose
here on this line, would you? That's it, thank you, well done,
well done. / How are the wickets today? / [SOUND OF
A COUGH] / Now close your— / Is my finger going up
or— / Can you feel this? / Can you feel this? / Name
something that grows on trees. / Who fixes teeth? /
What room do you cook in? / What year is this? / How
long have you been here? / Are we being too rippled
shotgun? / Would you like a cup of tea? / What is Jim
short for? / Point to your shoulder. / No, your shoulder.
/ What do you do with a book? / Don't worry, the water's
warm. We're holding you, don't worry. In we go, that's a girl!

AND THEN, AS SUDDENLY AS THE ASSAULT BEGAN, IT
IS OVER.

ONCE AGAIN, MRS. STILSON ALL ALONE ON STAGE,
DARKNESS ALL AROUND HER, NO SENSE OF WALLS OR
FURNITURE. UTTER ISOLATION.

MRS. STILSON [TRYING HARD TO KEEP SMILING]: *Yes,
all in all I'd say while things could be better could be worse,
far worse, how? Not quite sure. Just a sense I have. The sort
of sense that only great experience can mallees or rake,
plake I mean, flake . . . Drake! That's it.*

SHE STARES INTO SPACE.

SILENCE.

IN THE DISTANCE BEHIND HER, TWO DOCTORS
APPEAR.

FIRST DOCTOR: Mrs. Stilson, who was the first President of
the United States?

MRS. STILSON: *Washington.*

PAUSE.

SECOND DOCTOR [SPEAKING MORE SLOWLY THAN THE
FIRST DOCTOR DID; PERHAPS SHE SIMPLY DIDN'T HEAR
THE QUESTION]: Mrs. Stilson, who was the first President of
the United States?

MRS. STILSON: *Washington!*

SECOND DOCTOR [TO FIRST]: I don't think she hears
herself.

FIRST DOCTOR: No, I don't think she hears herself.

THE TWO DOCTORS EMERGE FROM THE SHADOWS,
APPROACH MRS. STILSON. SHE LOOKS UP IN TERROR.
THIS SHOULD BE THE FIRST TIME THAT THE WOMAN
ON STAGE HAS BEEN DIRECTLY FACED OR
CONFRONTED BY THE HOSPITAL STAFF. HER INNER
AND OUTER WORLDS ARE BEGINNING TO COME
TOGETHER.

FIRST DOCTOR: Mrs. Stilson, makey your naming powers?

MRS. STILSON: What?

SECOND DOCTOR: Canju spokeme?

MRS. STILSON: Can I what?

FIRST DOCTOR: Can do peeperear?

MRS. STILSON: *Don't believe what's going on!*

SECOND DOCTOR: Ahwill.

FIRST DOCTOR: Pollycadjis.

SECOND DOCTOR: Sewyladda?

FIRST DOCTOR [WITH A NOD]: Hm-hm.

EXIT DOCTORS.

MRS. STILSON [ALONE AGAIN]: *How it came to pass that I was captured!* [SHE PONDERS] *Hard to say really. I'll come back to that.*

PAUSE.

The room that I've been put in this time is quite small, square, what does square mean? . . . Means . . .

SENSE OF TIME PASSING. THE LIGHTS SHIFT. THE SPACE SHE IS IN BEGINS TO CHANGE ITS SHAPE.

Of course morning comes I think . . . [SHE PONDERS] *Yes, and night of course comes . . .* [PONDERS MORE] *Though sometimes . . .*

MRS. STILSON SOME PLACE ELSE NOW. AND SHE IS AWARE OF IT.

Yes, the way the walls choose to move around me . . . Yes, I've noticed that, I'm no fool!

A NURSE APPEARS CARRYING A DAZZLING BOUQUET OF FLOWERS. THIS BOUQUET IS THE FIRST REAL

COLOR WE HAVE SEEN.

NURSE: Good morning! Look what somebody's just sent you!
[SHE SETS THEM ON A TABLE] Wish I had as many
admirers as you.

EXIT NURSE, SMILING WARMLY.

MRS. STILSON'S EYES ARE DRAWN TO THE FLOWERS.
AND SOMETHING ABOUT THEM APPARENTLY RENDERS
IT IMPOSSIBLE FOR HER TO SHIFT HER GAZE AWAY.
SOMETHING ABOUT THESE FLOWERS HAS HER IN
THEIR THRALL.

WHAT IT IS IS THEIR COLOR.

IT IS AS IF SHE HAS NEVER EXPERIENCED COLOR
BEFORE. AND THE EXPERIENCE IS SO OVERWHELMING,
BOTH PHYSIOLOGICALLY AND PSYCHOLOGICALLY,
THAT HER BRAIN CANNOT PROCESS ALL THE
INFORMATION. HER CIRCUITRY IS OVERLOADED. IT IS
TOO MUCH SENSORY INPUT FOR HER TO HANDLE. AN
EXPLOSION IS IMMINENT. IF SOMETHING DOES NOT
INTERVENE TO DIVERT HER ATTENTION, MRS. STILSON
WILL VERY LIKELY FAINT, PERHAPS EVEN SUFFER A
SEIZURE.

A NARROW BEAM OF LIGHT, GROWING STEADILY IN
INTENSITY, FALLS UPON THE BOUQUET OF FLOWERS,
CAUSING THEIR COLORS TO TAKE ON AN INTENSITY
THEMSELVES THAT THEY OTHERWISE WOULD LACK. AT
THE SAME TIME, A SINGLE MUSICAL TONE IS HEARD,
VOLUME INCREASING.

A NURSE ENTERS THE ROOM.

NURSE: May I get you something?

MRS. STILSON [ABSTRACTED, EYES REMAINING ON THE
FLOWERS]: Yes, a sweater.

NURSE: Yes, of course. Think we have one here. [THE
NURSE OPENS A DRAWER, TAKES OUT A PILLOW,
HANDS THE PILLOW TO MRS. STILSON] Here.

MRS. STILSON ACCEPTS THE PILLOW
UNQUESTIONINGLY, EYES NEVER LEAVING THE
FLOWERS. SHE LAYS THE PILLOW ON HER LAP,
PROMPTLY FORGETS ABOUT IT. THE MUSICAL TONE
AND THE BEAM OF LIGHT CONTINUE RELENTLESSLY
TOWARD THEIR PEAK.

THE NURSE, OBLIVIOUS OF ANY CRISIS, EXITS.

THE SINGLE TONE AND THE BEAM OF LIGHT CREST
TOGETHER.

SILENCE FOLLOWS. THE BEAM DISAPPEARS. THE
FLOWERS SEEM NORMAL. THE LIGHTS AROUND MRS.
STILSON RETURN TO THE WAY THEY WERE BEFORE
THE GIFT OF FLOWERS WAS BROUGHT IN.

MRS. STILSON [SHAKEN]: *This is not a hospital of course,
and I know it! What it is is a farmhouse made up to look like
a hospital. Why? I'll come back to that.*

ENTER ANOTHER NURSE.

NURSE: Hi! Haven't seen you in a while. Have you missed
me?

MRS. STILSON [NO HINT OF RECOGNITION VISIBLE]:
What?

NURSE [WARMLY]: They say you didn't touch your dinner.
Would you like some pudding?

MRS. STILSON: No.

NURSE: Good, I'll go get you some.

EXIT NURSE, VERY CHEERFULLY.

MRS. STILSON: *Yes no question they have got me I've been what that word was captured is it? No it's—Yes, it's captured how? Near as it can figure. I was in my prane and crashed, not unusual, still in all not too common. Neither is it very grub. Plexit rather or I'd say propopic. Well that's that, jungdaball! Anyhow to resume, what I had for lunch? That's not it, good books I have read, good what, done what? Whaaaaat? Do the busy here! Get inside this, rubbidge all around let the vontul do some yes off or it of above semilacrum pwooosh! what with noddygobbit nip-n-crashing inside outside witsit watchit funnel vortex sucking-into backlash watchit get-out caught-in spinning ring-grab grobbit help woooosh! cannot stoppit on its own has me where it wants* [AND SUDDENLY SHE IS IN ANOTHER REALM. LIGHTS TRANSFORMED INTO WEIGHTLESS BLUE. SENSE OF EASE AND SERENITY] *Plane! See it thanks, okay, onto back we were and here it is. Slow down easy now. Captured. After crashing, that is what we said or was about to, think it so, cannot tell for sure, slow it slow it, okay here we go . . .* [SPEAKING SLOWER NOW] *captured after crashing by the enemy and brought here to this farm masquerading as a hospital. Why? For I would say offhand information. Of what sort though hard to tell. For example, questions such as can I raise my fingers, what's an overcoat, how many nickels in a rhyme, questions such as these. To what use can they be to the enemy? Hard to tell from here. Nonetheless, I would say must be certain information I possess that they want well I won't give it I'll escape! Strange things happen to me that they do! Good thing I'm all right! Must be in Rumania. Just a hunch of course.* [THE SERENE BLUE LIGHT STARTS TO FADE] *Ssssh, someone's coming.*

A NURSE HAS ENTERED. THE NURSE GUIDES MRS. STILSON TO A DOCTOR. THE BLUE LIGHT IS GONE. THE NURSE LEAVES.

THE SPACE MRS. STILSON NOW IS IN APPEARS MUCH

MORE "REAL" AND LESS FRAGMENTARY THAN WHAT
WE HAVE SO FAR BEEN OBSERVING. WE SEE MRS.
STILSON HERE AS OTHERS SEE HER.

DOCTOR: Mrs. Stilson, if you don't mind, I'd like to ask you
some questions. Some will be easy, some will be hard. Is
that all right?

MRS. STILSON: Oh yes I'd say oh well yes that's the twither
of it.

DOCTOR: Good. Okay. Where were you born?

MRS. STILSON: Never. Not at all. Here the match wundles
up you know and drats flames fires I keep careful always—

DOCTOR: Right . . . [SPEAKING VERY SLOWLY, PRECISE
ENUNCIATION] Where were you born?

MRS. STILSON: Well now well now that's a good thing
knowing yushof course wouldn't call it such as I did
andinjurations or aplovia could it? No I wouldn't think so.
Next?

PAUSE.

DOCTOR: Mrs. Stilson, are there seven days in a week?

MRS. STILSON: . . . Seven . . . Yes.

DOCTOR: Are there five days in a week?

PAUSE.

MRS. STILSON [AFTER MUCH PONDERING]: No.

DOCTOR: Can a stone float on water?

LONG PAUSE.

MRS. STILSON: No.

DOCTOR: Mrs. Stilson, can you cough?

MRS. STILSON: Somewhat.

DOCTOR: Well, would you show me how you cough?

MRS. STILSON: Well now well now not so easy what you cromplie is to put these bushes open and—

DOCTOR: No no, Mrs. Stilson, I'm sorry—I would like to hear you cough.

MRS. STILSON: Well I'm not bort you know with plajits or we'd see it wencherday she brings its pillow with the fistils-opening I'd say outward always outward never stopping it.

LONG SILENCE.

DOCTOR: Mrs. Stilson, I have some objects here. [HE TAKES A COMB, A TOOTHBRUSH, A PACK OF MATCHES, AND A KEY FROM HIS POCKET, SETS THEM DOWN WHERE SHE CAN SEE] Could you point to the object you would use for cleaning your teeth?

VERY LONG SILENCE.

FINALLY SHE PICKS UP THE COMB AND SHOWS IT TO HIM. THEN SHE PUTS IT DOWN. WAITS.

Mrs. Stilson, here, take this object in your hand. [HE HANDS HER THE TOOTHBRUSH] Do you know what this object is called?

MRS. STILSON [WITH GREAT DIFFICULTY]: Tooooooooovvvv . . . bbbrum?

DOCTOR: Very good. Now put it down.

SHE PUTS IT DOWN.

Now, pretend you have it in your hand. Show me what you'd do with it.

SHE DOES NOTHING.

What does one do with an object such as that, Mrs. Stilson?

NO RESPONSE.

Mrs. Stilson, what is the name of the object you are looking at?

MRS. STILSON: Well it's . . . wombly and not at all . . . rigged or tuned like we might twunter or toring to work the clambness out of it or—

DOCTOR: Pick it up.

MRS. STILSON [AS SOON AS SHE'S PICKED IT UP]: Tooovebram, tooove-britch bratch brush bridge, two-bridge.

DOCTOR: Show me what you do with it.

FOR SEVERAL MOMENTS SHE DOES NOTHING.

THEN SHE PUTS IT TO HER LIPS, HOLDS IT THERE MOTIONLESS.

Very good. Thank you.

SHE SIGHS HEAVILY, PUTS IT DOWN.

THE DOCTOR GATHERS UP HIS OBJECTS, LEAVES.

ONCE AGAIN MRS. STILSON ALL ALONE.

SHE STARES INTO SPACE.

THEN HER VOICE IS HEARD COMING FROM ALL
AROUND; SHE HERSELF DOES NOT SPEAK.

HER VOICE: *Dark now again out the window on my side
lying here all alone . . .*

VERY LONG SILENCE.

MRS. STILSON: *Yesterday my children came to see me.*

PAUSE.

*Or at least, I was told they were my children. Never saw
them before in my life.*

SHE STARES OUT, MOTIONLESS. NO EXPRESSION.

THEN AFTER A WHILE SHE LOOKS AROUND. STUDIES
THE DARK FOR CLUES.

Time has become peculiar.

AND SHE CONTINUES THIS SCRUTINY OF THE DARK.

BUT IF THIS ACTIVITY STEMS FROM CURIOSITY, IT IS A
MILD CURIOSITY AT MOST. NO LONGER DOES SHE
CONVEY OR PROBABLY EVEN EXPERIENCE THE
EXTREME, DISORIENTED DREAD WE SAW EARLIER
WHEN SHE FIRST ARRIVED IN THIS NEW REALM. HER
SENSE OF URGENCY IS GONE. INDEED, WERE WE ABLE
TO OBSERVE MRS. STILSON CONSTANTLY, WE WOULD
INEVITABLY CONCLUDE THAT HER CURIOSITY IS NOW
ONLY MINIMALLY PURPOSEFUL; THAT, IN FACT, MORE
LIKELY HER INVESTIGATIONS ARE THE ACTIONS,
POSSIBLY MERELY THE REFLEX ACTIONS, OF SOMEONE
WITH LITTLE OR NOTHING ELSE TO DO.

THIS IS NOT TO DENY THAT SHE IS DESPERATELY
TRYING TO PIECE HER SHATTERED WORLD TOGETHER.
UNDOUBTEDLY, IT IS THE DOMINANT MOTIF IN HER

MIND. BUT IT IS A MOTIF PROBABLY MORE ABSENT
FROM HER CONSCIOUSNESS THAN PRESENT, AND THE
QUEST IT INSPIRES IS INTERMITTENT AT BEST. HER
MENTAL ABILITIES HAVE NOT ONLY BEEN SEVERELY
ALTERED, THEY HAVE BEEN DIMINISHED: THAT IS THE
TERRIBLE FACT ONE CANNOT DENY.

AND THEN SUDDENLY SHE IS AGITATED.

Mother! . . . didn't say as she usually . . .

PAUSE.

*And I thought late enough or early rather first light coming so
when didn't move I poked her then with shoving but she
didn't even eyes or giggle when I tickled.*

PAUSE.

What it was was not a trick as I at first had—

PAUSE.

*Well I couldn't figure, he had never lied, tried to get her hold
me couldn't it was useless. Then his face was, I had never
known a face could . . . It was like a mask then like sirens it
was bursting open it was him then I too joining it was
useless. Can still feel what it was like when she held me.*

PAUSE.

*So then well I was on my own. He was all destroyed, had I
think they say no strength for this.*

THEN SHE'S SILENT. NO EXPRESSION. STARES INTO
SPACE.

ENTER A DOCTOR AND A NURSE.

DOCTOR [WARMLY]: Hello, Mrs. Stilson.

HE COMES OVER NEXT TO HER. WE CANNOT TELL IF
SHE NOTICES HIM OR NOT. THE NURSE, CHART IN
HAND, STANDS A SLIGHT DISTANCE AWAY.

You're looking much, much better. [HE SMILES AND SITS
DOWN NEXT TO HER. HE WATCHES HER FOR SEVERAL
MOMENTS, SEARCHING FOR SIGNS OF RECOGNITION]
Mrs. Stilson, do you know why you're here?

MRS. STILSON: Well now well now . . .

SHE GIVES IT UP.

SILENCE.

DOCTOR: You have had an accident—

MRS. STILSON: [HER WORDS OVERPOWERING HIS]	DOCTOR: [TO ALL INTENTS AND PURPOSES, WHAT HE SAYS IS LOST]
I don't trust him, don't trust anyone. Must get word out, send a message where I am. Like a wall between me and others. No one ever gets it right even though I tell them right. They are playing tricks on me, two sides, both not my friends, goes in goes out too fast too fast hurts do the busy I'm all right I talk right why acting all these others like I don't, what's he marking, what's he writing?	At home. Not in an airplane. It's called a stroke. This means that your brain has been injured and brain tissue destroyed, though we are not certain of the cause. You could get better, and you're certainly making progress. But it's still too soon to give any sort of exact prognosis. [HE STUDIES HER. THEN HE RISES AND MARKS SOMETHING ON HIS CLIPBOARD]

EXIT DOCTOR AND NURSE.

MRS. STILSON: *I am doing well of course!*

PAUSE.

[SECRETIVE TONE] *They still pretend they do not understand me. I believe they may be mad.*

PAUSE.

No they're not mad, I am mad. Today I heard it. Everything I speak is wronged. SOMETHING HAS BEEN DONE TO ME!

DOCTOR [BARELY VISIBLE IN THE DISTANCE]: Mrs. Stilson, can you repeat this phrase: "We live across the street from the school."

SHE PONDERS.

MRS. STILSON: "Malacats on the forturay are the kesterfats of the romancers."

LOOK OF HORROR COMES ACROSS HER FACE; THE DOCTOR VANISHES.

THROUGH THE SCREENS, UPSTAGE, WE SEE A NURSE BRINGING ON A TRAY OF FOOD.

NURSE [BRIGHTLY]: Okay ups-a-girl, ups-a-baby, dinnertime! Open wide now, mustn't go dribble-dribble—at's-a-way!

MRS. STILSON SCREAMS, SWINGS HER ARMS IN FURY. IN THE DISTANCE, UPSTAGE, THE TRAY OF FOOD GOES FLYING.

MRS. STILSON [SCREAMING]: Out! Get out! Take this shit away, I don't want it! Someone get me out of here!

NURSE [WHILE MRS. STILSON CONTINUES SHOUTING]: Help, someone, come quick! She's talking! Good as you or me! It's a miracle! Help! Somebody! Come quick!

WHILE MRS. STILSON CONTINUES TO SCREAM AND

FLAIL HER ARMS, NURSES AND DOCTORS RUSH ON
UPSTAGE AND SURROUND THE PATIENT WE NEVER
SEE.

AND ALTHOUGH MRS. STILSON CONTINUES TO SCREAM
COHERENTLY, IN FACT SHE ISN'T ANY BETTER, NO
MIRACLE HAS OCCURRED. HER ABILITY TO ARTICULATE
WITH APPARENT NORMALCY HAS BEEN BROUGHT ON
BY EXTREME AGITATION AND IN NO WAY IMPLIES THAT
SHE COULD PRODUCE THESE SOUNDS AGAIN "IF SHE
ONLY WANTED"; WILL POWER HAS NOTHING TO DO
WITH WHAT WE HEAR.

HER LANGUAGE, AS IT MUST, SOON SLIPS BACK INTO
JARGON. SHE CONTINUES TO FLAIL HER ARMS. IN THE
BACKGROUND, WE CAN SEE A NURSE PREPARING A
HYPODERMIC.

MRS. STILSON [STRUGGLING]:—flubdgy please
no-mommy-callming holdmeplease to sleeEEEEP SHOOOOP
shop shnoper CRROOOOOCK SNANNNNG wuduitcoldly
should I gobbin flutter truly HELP ME yessisnofun, snofun,
wishes awhin dahd killminsilf if . . . could [IN THE
DISTANCE, WE SEE THE NEEDLE GIVEN] OW! . . . would I
but . . . [SHE'S BECOMING DROWSY] . . . awful to me him
as well moas of all no cantduit . . . jusscantduit . . .

HEAD DROPS.

INTO SLEEP SHE GOES.

EXIT DOCTORS, NURSES.

SOUND OF A GENTLE WIND IS HEARD.

LIGHTS FADE TO BLACK ON MRS. STILSON.

DARKNESS EVERYWHERE; THE SOUND OF THE WIND
FADES AWAY.

SILENCE.

LIGHTS UP ON AMY, DOWNSTAGE RIGHT.

THEN LIGHTS UP ON MRS. STILSON STARING INTO
SPACE.

AMY: Mrs. Stilson?

MRS. STILSON TURNS TOWARD THE SOUND, SEES AMY.

You have had what's called a stroke.

CHANGE OF LIGHTS AND PANELS OPEN. SENSE OF
TERRIBLE ENCLOSURE GONE. BIRDS HEARD. WE ARE
OUTSIDE NOW. AMY PUTS A SHAWL AROUND MRS.
STILSON'S SHOULDERS.

AMY: Are you sure that will be enough?

MRS. STILSON: Oh yes . . . thhhankyou.

SHE TUCKS THE SHAWL AROUND HERSELF.

THEN AMY GUIDES HER THROUGH THE PANELS AS IF
THROUGH CORRIDORS; NO RUSH, SLOW GENTLE
STROLL.

THEY EMERGE OTHER SIDE OF STAGE. WARM LIGHT.
AMY TAKES IN THE VIEW. MRS. STILSON APPEARS
INDIFFERENT.

AMY: Nice to be outside, isn't it? . . . Nice view.

MRS. STILSON [STILL WITH INDIFFERENCE]: Yes indeed.

THERE ARE TWO CHAIRS NEARBY, AND THEY SIT.

SILENCE FOR A TIME.

AMY: Are you feeling any better today?

BUT SHE GETS NO RESPONSE.

THEN, A MOMENT LATER, MRS. STILSON TURNS TO
AMY; IT IS AS IF AMY'S QUESTION HAS NOT EVEN BEEN
HEARD.

MRS. STILSON: The thing is . . .

BUT THE STATEMENT TRAILS OFF INTO NOTHINGNESS.

SHE STARES OUT, NO EXPRESSION.

AMY: Yes? What?

LONG SILENCE.

MRS. STILSON: I can't make it do it like it used to.

AMY: Yes, I know. That's because of the accident.

MRS. STILSON [SEEMINGLY OBLIVIOUS OF AMY'S
WORDS]: The words, they go in somelimes then out they go,
I can't stop them here inside or make maybe globbidge to
the tubberway or—

AMY: Emily. Emily!

MRS. STILSON [SHAKEN OUT OF HERSELF]: . . . What?

AMY: Did you hear what you just said?

MRS. STILSON: . . . Why?

AMY [SPEAKING SLOWLY]: You must listen to what you're
saying.

MRS. STILSON: Did I . . . do . . .

AMY [NODDING, SMILING; CLEARLY NO REPROACH
INTENDED]: Slow down. Listen to what you're saying.

SILENCE.

MRS. STILSON [SLOWER]: The thing is . . . doing all this
busy in here gets, you know with the talking it's like . . .
sometimes when I hear here [SHE TOUCHES HER HEAD]
. . . but when I start to . . . kind more what kind of voice
should . . . it's like pfffft! [SHE MAKES A GESTURE WITH
HER HAND OF SOMETHING FLYING AWAY]

AMY [SMILING]: Yes, I know. It's hard to find the words for
what you're thinking of.

MRS. STILSON: Well yes.

LONG PAUSE.

And then these people, they keep waiting . . . And I see
they're smiling and . . . they keep . . . waiting . . .[FAINT
SMILE, HELPLESS GESTURE. SHE STARES OFF]

LONG SILENCE.

AMY: Emily.

MRS. STILSON LOOKS UP.

Can you remember anything about your life . . . before the
accident?

MRS. STILSON: Not sometimes, some days it goes better if I
see a thing or smell . . . it . . . remembers me back, you see?
And I see things that maybe they were me and maybe they
were just some things you know that happens in the night
when you . . . [STRUGGLING VISIBLY] have your things
closed, eyes.

AMY: A dream you mean.

MRS. STILSON [WITH RELIEF]: Yes. So I don't know for
sure.

PAUSE.

If it was really me.

LONG SILENCE.

AMY: Your son is bringing a picture of you when you were
younger. We thought you might like that.

NO VISIBLE RESPONSE. LONG SILENCE.

You used to fly, didn't you?

MRS. STILSON [BRIGHTLY]: Oh yes indeed! Very much! I
walked . . . out . . .

PAUSE.

[SOFTLY, PROUDLY] I walked out on wings.

LIGHTS FADE ON AMY. MRS. STILSON ALONE AGAIN.

*Sitting here on my bed I can close my eyes shut out all that I
can't do with, hearing my own talking, others, names that
used to well just be there when I wanted now all somewhere
else. No control. Close my eyes then, go to—*

SOUND OF SOMETHING FLAPPING RAPIDLY.

A FIBRILLATION.

LIGHTS BECOME BLUE. SENSE OF WEIGHTLESSNESS,
SERENITY.

*Here I go. No one talks here. Images coming I seem feel it
feels better this way here is how it goes: this time I am still in
the middle Stilson in the middle going out walking out wind
feels good hold the wires feel the hum down below far there*

*they are now we turn it bank it now we spin! Looks more bad
than really is, still needs good balance and those nerves and
that thing that courage thing don't fall off!* . . . *And now I'm
out* . . . *and back and* . . . [WITH SURPRISE] *there's the
window.*

LIGHTS HAVE RETURNED TO NORMAL. SHE IS BACK
WHERE SHE STARTED.

AMY ENTERS.

AMY: Hello, Emily.

MRS. STILSON: Oh, Amy! . . . Didn't hear what you was . . .
coming here to . . . Oh!

AMY: What is it?

MRS. STILSON: Something . . . wet.

AMY: Do you know what it is?

MRS. STILSON: Don't . . . can't say find it word.

AMY: Try. You can find it.

MRS. STILSON: Wet . . . thing, many, both sides yes.

AMY: Can you name them? What they are? You do know
what they are.

PAUSE.

MRS. STILSON: . . . Tears?

AMY: That's right, very good. Those are tears. And do you
know what that means?

MRS. STILSON: . . . Sad?

AMY: Yes, right, well done, it means . . . that you are sad.

Explorations

STAGE DARK.

IN THE DARK, A PIANO HEARD: SOMEONE FOOLING
AROUND ON THE KEYBOARD, BRIEF HALTING
SNATCHES OF OLD SONGS EMERGING AS THE
PRODUCT; WOULD CONSTITUTE A MEDLEY WERE THE
SEGMENTS ONLY LONGER, MORE COHESIVE. AS IT IS,
SUSPICION AROUSED THAT WHAT WE HEAR IS ALL THE
PIANIST CAN REMEMBER.

SOUND OF GENERAL LAUGHTER, HUBBUB.

LIGHTS RISE.

WHAT WE SEE IS A REC ROOM, IN SOME PLACES
CLEARLY, IN OTHERS NOT (THE ROOM BEING
OBSERVED PARTLY THROUGH THE DARK SCRIM
PANELS).

UPSTAGE RIGHT, AN UPRIGHT PIANO, PLAYERS AND
FRIENDS GATHERED ROUND. DOCTORS, THERAPISTS,
NURSES, ATTENDANTS, PATIENTS, VISITORS CERTAINLY
ARE NOT ALL SEEN, BUT THOSE WE DO SEE COME
FROM SUCH A GROUP. WE ARE IN THE REC ROOM OF
A REHABILITATION CENTER. SOME PATIENTS IN
WHEELCHAIRS.

THE ROOM ITSELF HAS BRIGHT COMFORTABLE CHAIRS,
PERHAPS A CARD TABLE, MAGAZINE RACK, CERTAINLY
A TV SET. SOMEONE NOW TURNS ON THE TV.

WHAT EMERGES IS THE SOUND OF ELLA FITZGERALD
IN LIVE PERFORMANCE. SHE SINGS SCAT: MELLOW,
UPBEAT.

THE PATIENTS AND STAFF PERSUADE THE PIANIST TO
CEASE. ELLA'S RIFFS OF SCAT CAST SOMETHING LIKE
A SPELL.

MRS. STILSON WANDERS THROUGH THE SPACE.

THE REC ROOM, IT SHOULD BE STRESSED, SHOWS
MORE DETAIL AND COLOR THAN ANY SPACE WE'VE SO
FAR SEEN. PERHAPS A VASE OF FLOWERS HELPS TO
SIGNAL THAT MRS. STILSON'S WORLD IS BECOMING
FULLER, MORE INTEGRATED.

MOVEMENTS TOO SEEM NORMAL, SAME FOR
CONVERSATIONS THAT GO ON DURING ALL OF THIS,
THOUGH TOO SOFTLY FOR US TO COMPREHEND.

THE MUSIC OF COURSE SETS THE TONE. ALL WHO
LISTEN ARE IN ITS THRALL.

NEW TIME SENSE HERE, A LANGUOR ALMOST. THE
DREAD MRS. STILSON FELT HAS BEEN REPLACED BY
AN ACKNOWLEDGMENT OF HER CONDITION, THOUGH
NOT AN UNDERSTANDING.

IN THIS TIME BEFORE SHE SPEAKS, AND IN FACT
DURING, WE OBSERVE THE LIFE OF THE REC ROOM
BEHIND AND AROUND HER. THIS IS NOT A HOSPITAL
ANY MORE, AND A KIND OF NORMALCY PREVAILS.

THE SENSE SHOULD BE CONVEYED OF CORRIDORS
LEADING TO AND FROM THIS ROOM.

THEN THE MUSIC AND THE REC ROOM SOUNDS GROW
DIM; MRS. STILSON COMES FORWARD, LOST IN THE
DRIFTS OF A THOUGHT.

MRS. STILSON [RELAXED, MELLOW]: *Wonder . . . what's
inside of it . . .?*

PAUSE.

*I mean, how does it work? What's inside that . . . makes it
work?*

LONG PAUSE. SHE PONDERS.

I mean when you . . . think about it all . . .

PAUSE.

*And when you think that it could . . . ever have been . . .
possible to . . . be another way . . .*

SHE PONDERS.

BUT IT'S HARD FOR HER TO KEEP IN MIND WHAT SHE'S
BEEN THINKING OF, AND SHE HAS TO FIGHT THE NOISE
OF THE REC ROOM, ITS INTRUSIVE PRESENCE. LIKE A
NOVICE JUGGLER, MRS. STILSON IS UNABLE TO KEEP
OUTSIDE IMAGES AND INNER THOUGHTS GOING
SIMULTANEOUSLY. WHEN SHE'S WITH HER THOUGHTS,
THE OUTSIDE WORLD FADES AWAY. WHEN THE
OUTSIDE WORLD IS WITH HER, HER THOUGHTS FADE
AWAY.

BUT SHE FIGHTS HER WAY THROUGH IT, AND KEEPS
THE THOUGHT IN MIND.

THE REC ROOM, WHOSE NOISE HAS JUST INCREASED,
GROWS QUIET.

Maybe . . . if somehow I could— [SHE SEARCHES FOR
THE WORDS THAT MATCH HER CONCEPT]—*get inside . . .*

PAUSE.

SOUNDS OF THE REC ROOM PULSE LOUDER. SHE
FIGHTS AGAINST IT. THE REC ROOM SOUNDS DIMINISH.

Prob'ly . . . very dark inside . . . [SHE PONDERS; TRIES TO
PICTURE WHAT SHE'S THINKING] *Yes . . . twisting kind of
place I bet . . .* [PONDERS MORE] *With lots of . . .* [SHE
SEARCHES FOR THE PROPER WORD; FINDS IT] . . .
passageways that . . . lead to . . . [AGAIN, SHE SEARCHES
FOR THE WORD]

THE OUTSIDE WORLD RUSHES IN.

PATIENT IN A WHEELCHAIR [ONLY BARELY AUDIBLE]:
My foot feels sour.

AN ATTENDANT PUTS A LAP RUG OVER THE PATIENT'S
LIMBS. THEN THE REC ROOM, ONCE AGAIN, FADES
AWAY.

MRS. STILSON [FIGHTING ON]: . . . *lead to . . . something
. . . Door! Yes . . . closed off now I . . . guess possib . . . ly
for good I mean . . . forever, what does that mean?* [SHE
PONDERS]

ATTENDANT: Would you like some candy?

MRS. STILSON: No.

ATTENDANT: Billy made it.

MRS. STILSON: No!

THE ATTENDANT MOVES BACK INTO THE SHADOWS.

Where was I? [SHE LOOKS AROUND] *Why can't they just
. . . let me . . . be when I'm . . .*

LIGHTS START TO CHANGE. HER WORLD SUDDENLY IN
FLUX. THE REC ROOM FADES FROM VIEW. SOUNDS OF
BIRDS HEARD, DIMLY AT FIRST.

[AWARE OF THE CHANGE AS IT IS OCCURRING] . . .
okay. Slipping out of . . . it and . . .

MRS. STILSON IN A DIFFERENT PLACE.

Outside now! How . . . did I do that?

AMY [EMERGING FROM THE SHADOWS]: Do you like this
new place better?

MRS. STILSON: Oh well oh well yes, much, all . . . nice flowers here, people seem . . . more like me Thank you.

AMY MOVES BACK TOWARD THE SHADOWS.

And then I see it happen once again . . .

AMY GONE FROM SIGHT.

Amy kisses me. Puts her—what thing is it, arm! yes, arm, puts her arm around my . . .

PAUSE.

. . . shoulder, turns her head away so I can't . . .

PAUSE.

Well, it knows what she's doing. May not get much better even though I'm here. No, I know that. I know that. No real need for her to . . .

LONG PAUSE.

Then she kisses me again.

PAUSE.

Walks away . . .

PAUSE.

LIGHTS CHANGE AGAIN, WORLD AGAIN IN FLUX. NOISES OF THE BUILDING'S INTERIOR CAN BE HEARD LIKE A BABEL, ONLY FLEETINGLY COHERENT. THE REC ROOM SEEN DISSOLVING.

MRS. STILSON: *Where am I?*

SHE BEGINS TO WANDER THROUGH A MAZE OF

PASSAGEWAYS. THE MIRRORS MULTIPLY HER IMAGE,
CREATE A SENSE OF ENDLESSNESS.

[*Note. The following blocks of sound, which accompany her
expedition, are meant to blend and overlap in performance
and, to that end, can be used in any order and combined in
any way desired, except for the last five blocks, numbers
12–16, which must be performed in their given sequence and
in a way that is comprehensible. The sounds themselves
may be live or pre-recorded; those which are pre-recorded
should emanate from all parts of the theater and in no
predictable pattern. The effect should be exhilarating and
disorienting. An adventure. With terrifying aspects to be sure.
But the sense of mystery and adventure must never be so
overwhelmed by the terror that it is either lost altogether or
submerged to the point of insignificance.*

*Mrs. Stilson may be frightened here, but the fear does not
prevent her from exploring.*

*She wanders through the labyrinth of dark panels as if they
were so many doors, each door leading into yet another
realm.*]

BLOCK 1: It was but a few years later that Fritsch and Hitzig
stimulated the cortex of a dog with an electric current. Here
at last was dramatic and indisputable evidence that—

BLOCK 2: Would you like me to change the channel?

BLOCK 3: . . . presented, I would say, essentially similar
conclusions on the behavioral correlates of each cerebral
convolution.

BLOCK 4 [BEING THE DEEP MALE VOICE, SPEAKING
SLOWLY, ENUNCIATING CAREFULLY, THAT ONE HEARS
ON THE SPEECH-THERAPY MACHINE KNOWN AS "THE
LANGUAGE MASTER"]: Mother led Bud to the bed.

BLOCK 5: . . . In the laboratory then, through electrical
stimulation of neural centers or excisions of areas of the

brain, scientists acquired information about the organization of mental activities in the monkey, the dog, the cat, and the rat. The discovery of certain peculiar clinical pictures, reminiscent of bizarre human syndromes, proved of special interest.

BLOCK 6: Can you tell me what this object's called?

BLOCK 7: ELLA'S RIFFS OF SCAT, AS IF WE WERE STILL IN THE REC ROOM AFTER ALL.

BLOCK 8: One has only to glance through the writings of this period to sense the heightened excitement attendant upon these discoveries!

BLOCK 9: Possibly some diaschisis, which would of course help account for the apparent mirroring. And then, of course, we must not overlook the fact that she's left-handed.

BLOCK 10: Of course, you understand, these theories may all be wrong! [SOUND OF LAUGHTER FROM AN AUDIENCE] Any other questions? Yes, over there, in the corner.

BLOCK 11: Mrs. Stilson, this is Dr. Rogans. Dr. Rogans, this is Emily Stilson.

BLOCK 12: MALE VOICE: —definite possibility I would say of a tiny subclinical infarct in Penfield's area. Yes? FEMALE VOICE: Are you sure there is a Penfield's area? MALE VOICE: No. [LAUGHTER FROM HIS AUDIENCE] MALE VOICE AGAIN [ITSELF ON THE VERGE OF LAUGHTER]: But *something* is wrong with her! [RAUCOUS LAUGHTER FROM HIS AUDIENCE]

[*Note. Emerging out of the laughter in Block 12, a single musical TONE. This tone increases in intensity. It should carry through Block 16 and into Mrs. Stilson's emergence from the maze of panels, helping to propel her into the realm and the memory to which this expedition has been leading.*]

BLOCK 13: The controversy, of course, is that some feel it's
language without thought, and others, thought without
language . . .

BLOCK 14: What it is, of course, is the symbol system. Their
symbol system's shot. They can't make analogies.

BLOCK 15: You see, it's all so unpredictable. There are no
fixed posts, no clear boundaries. The victim, you could say,
has been cut adrift . . .

BLOCK 16: Ah, now you're really flying blind there!

MRS. STILSON EMERGES FROM THE MAZE OF
CORRIDORS. SOUND PERHAPS OF WIND, OR BELLS.
LIGHTS BLUE, SENSE AGAIN OF WEIGHTLESSNESS,
AIRINESS.

MRS. STILSON [IN AWE AND ECSTASY]: *As I see it now,
the plane was flying BACKWARDS! Really, wind that strong,
didn't know it could be! Yet the sky was clear, not a cloud,
crystal blue, gorgeous, angels could've lived in sky like that
. . . I think the cyclone must've blown in on the Andes from
the sea . . .*

BLUE LIGHT FADES. WIND GONE, BELLS GONE,
MUSICAL TONE IS GONE.

[COMING OUT OF IT] *Yes* . . . [SHE LOOKS AROUND;
GETS HER BEARINGS] *Yes, no question, this . . . place
better.* [AND NOW SHE'S LANDED] *All these people just . . .
like me, I guess.*

SHE TAKES IN WHERE SHE IS, SEEMS SLIGHTLY
STUNNED TO BE BACK WHERE SHE STARTED. SENSE
OF WONDERMENT APPARENT.

AN ATTENDANT APPROACHES.

ATTENDANT: Mrs. Stilson?

MRS. STILSON [STARTLED]: Oh!

ATTENDANT: Sorry to—

MRS. STILSON: Is it . . . ?

ATTENDANT: Yes.

MRS. STILSON: Did I . . . ?

ATTENDANT: No, no need to worry. Here, I'll take you.

THE ATTENDANT GUIDES MRS. STILSON TO A THERAPY ROOM, THOUGH, IN FACT, MORE LIKELY (ON THE STAGE) THE ROOM ASSEMBLES AROUND HER. IN THE ROOM ARE AMY, BILLY (A MAN IN HIS MIDDLE THIRTIES), MRS. TIMMINS (ELDERLY, IN A WHEELCHAIR), AND MR. BROWNSTEIN (ALSO ELDERLY AND IN A WHEELCHAIR).

THE ATTENDANT LEAVES.

AMY: Well! Now that we're all here on this lovely afternoon, I thought that maybe—

BILLY: She looks really good.

AMY: What?

BILLY: This new lady here, can't remember what her name is, no bother, anyhow, she looks really nice all dressed like this, an' I jus' wanna extent a nice welcome here on behalf o' all of us.

THE OTHER PATIENTS MUMBLE THEIR ASSENT.

AMY: Well, that is very nice, Billy, very nice. Can any of the rest of you remember this woman's name?

BILLY: I seen her I think when it is, yesterday, how's that?

AMY: Very good, that's right, you met her for the first time yesterday. Now, can any of you remember her name?

BILLY: Dolores.

AMY [LAUGHING SLIGHTLY]: No, not Dolores.

MR. BROWNSTEIN: She vas, I caught sight ya know, jussaminute, flahtied or vhat, vhere, midda [HE HUMS A NOTE]—

AMY: Music.

MR. BROWNSTEIN: Yeah right goodgirlie right she vas lissning, I caught slight, saw her vooding bockstond tipping-n-topping de foot vas jussnow like dis. [HE STARTS TO STAMP HIS FOOT]

AMY: Mrs. Stilson, were you inside listening to some music just now?

MRS. STILSON: Well . . .

PAUSE.

[VERY FAST] Well now I was yes in the what in-the-in-the where the—

AMY [CHEERFULLY]: Sssssslllow dowwwwn.

THE OTHER PATIENTS LAUGH; MRS. TIMMINS SOFTLY ECHOES THE PHRASE "SLOW DOWN."

[SPEAKING VERY SLOWLY] Listen to yourself talking.

MRS. STILSON [SPEAKING SLOWLY]: Well yes, I was . . . listening and it was it was going in . . . good I think, I'd say, very good yes I liked it very nice it made it very nice inside.

AMY: Well, good.

MRS. TIMMINS: Applawdgia!

AMY: Ah, Mrs. Timmins! You heard the music, too?

MRS. TIMMINS [WITH A LAUGH]: Ohshorrrrrn. Yossssso, TV.

AMY: Well, good for you! Anyway, I'd like you all to know that this new person in our group is named Mrs. Stilson.

MR. BROWNSTEIN: Sssssstaa-illlllsssim.

AMY: Right! Well done, Mr. Brownstein!

MR. BROWNSTEIN [LAUGHING PROUDLY]: It's vurktiddiDINGobitch!

AMY: That's right it's working, I told you it would.

BILLY: Hey! Wait, hold on here—jus' remembered!

AMY: What's that, Billy?

BILLY: You've been holdin' out pay up where is it?

AMY: Where . . . is what?

BILLY: Where is for all what I did all that time labor which you—don't kid me, I see you grinning back there ate up [HE MAKES MUNCHING SOUNDS] so where is it, where's the loot?

AMY: For the cheesecake.

BILLY: That's right you know it for the cheesecape, own recipe, extra-special, pay up.

AMY [TO MRS. STILSON]: Billy is a terrific cook.

MRS. STILSON [DELIGHTED]: Oh!

BILLY: Well used t' be, not now much what they say, anyhow, hah-hah! see? look, laughing, giggles, tries t' hide it, she knows she knows, scoundrel, thief, can't sleep nights can you, people give their arms whatnots recipe like that one is. Cheapskate. Come on fork over hand it over, don't be chief.

AMY: . . . What?

BILLY: Don't be chief.

PAUSE.

You know, when someone don' pay, you say he's chief.

AMY [WARMLY, NEARLY LAUGHING]: Billy, you're not listening.

BILLY: Okay not the word not the right word what's the word? I'll take any help you can give me. [HE LAUGHS]

AMY: Cheap.

BILLY: That's it that's the word that's what you are, from now on I'm gonna sell my recipes somewheres else.

AMY: Billy, say cheap.

HE SIGHS MIGHTILY.

BILLY: . . . Chief.

HER EXPRESSION TELLS HIM EVERYTHING.

Not right okay, try again this thing we can, what's its, lessee okay here we go CHARF! Nope. Not right. Ya know really, this could take all day.

AMY: Well then, the sooner you do it, the sooner we can go on to what I've planned.

BILLY: You've got somethin' planned? You've never got somethin' planned.

AMY: I've *always* got something planned.

BILLY: Oh come on don' gimme that, you're jus' tryin' to impress this new lady, really nice new lady, Mrs. . . .

AMY: Stilson.

BILLY: Yeah her, you're jus' tryin'—what's that word again?

AMY: Cheap.

BILLY: Cheap right okay lessee now—

AMY: Billy! You just said it!

BILLY: Did I? Good. Then maybe we can go on to somethin' else, such as when you're gonna fork over for the cheesecake, I could be a rich man now.

AMY: Billy, I never made the cheesecake.

BILLY: I'll bet you've gone sold the recipe to all the stores the whatnot everywhere fancy bigdeal places made a fortune, gonna retire any day t' your farm in New Jersey.

AMY: I don't have a farm in New Jersey, *you* have a farm in New Jersey!

BILLY: Oh? Then what were you doin' on my farm then?

AMY: I wasn't on your farm, Billy, I've been here!
[BILLY STARTS ARGUING ABOUT SOMETHING INCOMPREHENSIBLE AND SEEMINGLY UNRELATED TO FARM LIFE, THE ARGUMENT CONSISTING MOSTLY OF THE RECITATION OF A CONVOLUTED STRING OF NUMBERS; AMY CUTS HIM SHORT BEFORE HE GOES TOO FAR ASTRAY] Billy, cheap, say cheap!

LONG SILENCE.

BILLY [SIMPLY AND WITHOUT EFFORT]: Cheap.

AMY CHEERS.

[OVERJOYED] Cheap!— Cheap-cheap-cheap-cheap-cheap!

MR. BROWNSTEIN: I vas hoping you could polsya and git vid mustard all dis out of dis you gottit right good I say hutchit and congratulupsy!

AMY: Congratu*lations.*

MR. BROWNSTEIN: Yeah right dassit goodgirlie, phhhhew! fin'lly!

LIGHTS FADE TO BLACK ALL AROUND MRS. STILSON. NOTHING SEEN BUT HER.

SILENCE FOR A TIME.

MRS. STILSON: *What it was . . . how I heard it how I said it not the same, you would think so but it's not. Sometimes . . . well it just goes in so fast, in-and-out all the sounds. I know they mean—*

PAUSE.

I mean I know they're . . . well like with me, helping, as their at their in their best way knowing how I guess they practice all the time so I'd say must be good or even better, helps me get the dark out just by going you know sssslowww and thinking smiling . . . it's not easy.

PAUSE.

Sometimes . . . how can . . . well it's just I think these death things, end it, stuff like sort of may be better not to listen anything no more at all or trying even talking cause what good's it, I'm so far away! Well it's crazy I don't mean it I don't think, still it's just like clouds that you can't push through. Still you do it, still you try to. I can't hear things same as others say them.

PAUSE.

So the death thing, it comes in, I don't ask it, it just comes in, plays around in there, I can't get it out till it's ready, goes out on its own. Same I guess for coming. I don't open up the door.

SILENCE.

LIGHTS UP ON A CHAIR, SMALL TABLE.

ON THE TABLE, A CASSETTE RECORDER.

MRS. STILSON GOES TO THE CHAIR. SITS. STARES AT THE RECORDER.

A FEW MOMENTS LATER, BILLY AND A DOCTOR ENTER.

BILLY: Oh, I'm sorry, I didn't know you was in . . . here or . . .

MRS. STILSON: Dr. Freedman said I could . . . use room and his . . . this . . . [SHE GESTURES TOWARD THE RECORDER]

DOCTOR: No problem, we'll use another room.

HE SMILES. EXIT BILLY AND DOCTOR.

MRS. STILSON TURNS BACK TO THE MACHINE. STARES AT IT. THEN SHE REACHES OUT, PRESSES A BUTTON.

DOCTOR'S VOICE [FROM CASSETTE RECORDER]: All right, essentially, a stroke occurs when there's a stoppage . . . When blood flow ceases in one part of the brain . . . And

that brain can no longer get oxygen . . . And subsequently
dies. Okay? Now, depending upon which part of the brain is
affected by the stroke, you'll see differences in symptoms.
Now what you've had is a left cerebral infarction. Oh, by the
way, you're doing much, much better. We were very worried
when you first arrived . . .

SILENCE.

SHE CLICKS OFF THE RECORDING MACHINE. DOES
NOTHING, STARES AT NOTHING. THEN SHE REACHES
OUT AND PUSHES THE REWIND BUTTON. THE MACHINE
REWINDS TO START OF TAPE. STOPS AUTOMATICALLY.
SHE STARES AT THE MACHINE. DEEP BREATH.
REACHES OUT AGAIN. PRESSES THE PLAYBACK
BUTTON.

DOCTOR'S VOICE: All right, essentially, a stroke occurs
when there's a stoppage . . . When blood flow ceases in one
part of the brain . . . And that brain can no long—

SHE SHUTS IT OFF.

STARES INTO SPACE.

SILENCE.

MRS. STILSON WITH AMY SITTING NEXT TO HER ON
ANOTHER CHAIR.

MRS. STILSON [STILL STARING INTO SPACE]:
"Memory" . . .

PAUSE.

AMY: Yes, come on, "memory" . . .

NO RESPONSE.

Anything.

STILL NO RESPONSE.

[WARMLY]: Oh, come on, I bet there are lots of things you can talk about . . . You've been going out a lot lately . . . With your son . . . With your niece . . .

PAUSE.

What about Rhinebeck? Tell me about Rhinebeck.

PAUSE.

MRS. STILSON: On . . . Saturday . . . [SHE PONDERS] On . . . Sunday my . . . son . . . [PONDERS AGAIN] On Saturday my son . . . took me to see them out at Rhinebeck.

AMY: See what?

MRS. STILSON: What I used to . . . fly in.

AMY: Can you think of the word?

MRS. STILSON: . . . What word?

AMY: For what you used to fly in.

LONG PAUSE.

MRS. STILSON: Planes!

AMY: Very good!

MRS. STILSON: Old . . . planes.

AMY: That is very good. Really!

MRS. STILSON: I sat . . . inside one of them. He said it was like the kind I used to . . . fly in and walk . . . out on wings in. I couldn't believe I could have ever done this.

PAUSE.

But he said I did, I had. He was very . . . proud.

PAUSE.

Then . . . I saw my hand was pushing on this . . . stick . . . Then my hand was . . . pulling. Well I hadn't you know asked my hand to do this, it just went and did it on its own. So I said okay Emily, if this is how it wants to do it you just sit back here and watch . . . But . . . my head, it was really . . . hurting bad. And I was up here both . . . sides, you know . . .

AMY: Crying.

MRS. STILSON [WITH EFFORT]: Yeah.

LONG PAUSE.

And then all at once—it remembered everything!

LONG PAUSE.

But now it doesn't.

SILENCE.

FAINT SOUND OF WIND. HINT OF BELLS.

THE SCREENS OPEN.

WE ARE OUTSIDE. SENSE OF DISTANCE, OPENNESS. ALL FEELING OF CONSTRAINT IS GONE. AMY HELPS MRS. STILSON INTO AN OVERCOAT; AMY IS IN AN OVERCOAT ALREADY.

AMY: Are you sure you'll be warm enough?

MRS. STILSON: Oh yes . . .

AND THEY START TO WALK—A LEISURELY STROLL THROUGH A PARK OR MEADOW, SENSE OF WHITENESS EVERYWHERE. THEY HEAD TOWARD A BENCH WITH SNOW ON ITS SLATS. THE SOUND OF WIND GROWS STRONGER.

FAINT SOUND OF AN AIRPLANE OVERHEAD, THE SOUND QUICKLY DISAPPEARING.

MRS. STILSON: This is winter, isn't it?

AMY: Yes.

MRS. STILSON: That was just a guess, you know.

AMY [WITH A WARM, EASY LAUGH]: Well, it was a good one, keep it up!

MRS. STILSON LAUGHS.

AMY STOPS BY THE BENCH.

Do you know what this is called?

MRS. STILSON: Bench!

AMY: Very good! No, I mean what's on top of it.

NO RESPONSE.

What I'm brushing off . . .

STILL NO RESPONSE.

What's falling from the sky . . .

LONG SILENCE.

MRS. STILSON: Where do you get names from?

AMY: I? From in here, same as you.

MRS. STILSON: Do you know how you do it?

AMY: No.

MRS. STILSON: Then how am I supposed . . . to learn?

AMY [SOFTLY]: I don't really know.

MRS. STILSON STARES AT AMY. THEN SHE POINTS AT
HER AND LAUGHS.

AT FIRST, AMY DOESN'T UNDERSTAND.

THEN SHE DOES.

AND THEN BOTH OF THEM ARE LAUGHING.

MRS. STILSON: Look. You see? [SHE SCOOPS SOME
SNOW OFF THE BENCH] If I pick this . . . stuff up in my
hand, then . . . I know its name. I didn't have to pick it up to
know . . . what it *was*.

AMY: No . . .

MRS. STILSON: But to find its name . . . [SHE STARES AT
WHAT IS IN HER HAND] I had to pick it up.

AMY: What's its name?

MRS. STILSON: Snow. It's really nuts, isn't it!

AMY: It's peculiar!

THEY LAUGH.

THEN, LAUGHTER GONE, THEY SIT; STARE OUT.

SILENCE FOR A TIME.

MRS. STILSON: A strange thing happened to me . . .

PAUSE.

I think last night.

AMY: Can you remember it?

MRS. STILSON: Perfectly.

AMY: Ah!

MRS. STILSON: I think it may have been . . . you know, when you sleep . . .

AMY: A dream.

MRS. STILSON: Yes, one of those, but I'm not . . . sure that it was . . . that.

PAUSE. THEN SHE NOTICES THE SNOW IN HER HAND.

Is it all right if I . . . eat this?

AMY: Yes! We used to make a ball of it, then pour maple syrup on top. Did you ever do that?

MRS. STILSON: I don't know.

PAUSE.

No, I remember—I did!

SHE TASTES THE SNOW. SMILES.

AFTER A TIME, THE SMILE VANISHES.

SHE TURNS BACK TO AMY.

Who was that man yesterday?

AMY: What man?

MRS. STILSON: In our group. He seemed all right.

AMY: Oh, that was last week.

MRS. STILSON: I thought for sure he was all right! I thought
he was maybe, you know, a doctor.

AMY: Yes, I know.

MRS. STILSON [SEARCHING HER MEMORY]: And you
asked him to show you where his . . . hand was.

AMY: And he knew.

MRS. STILSON: That's right, he raised his hand, he knew.
So I thought, why is Amy joking?

SHE PONDERS.

Then you asked him . . . [SHE TRIES TO REMEMBER] . . .
where . . . [SHE TURNS TO AMY]

AMY: His elbow was.

MRS. STILSON: Yes! And he . . . [SHE STRUGGLES TO
FIND THE WORD]

AMY [HELPING]: Pointed—

MRS. STILSON [AT THE SAME TIME]: Pointed! to . . .[BUT THE STRUGGLE'S GETTING HARDER]

AMY: The corner of the room.

MRS. STILSON: Yes.

PAUSE.

[SOFTLY] That was very . . . scary.

AMY: Yes.

MRS. STILSON STARES INTO SPACE.

SILENCE.

What is it that happened to you last night?

MRS. STILSON: Oh yes! Well, this . . . *person* . . . came into my room. I couldn't tell if it was a man or woman or . . . young or old. I was in my bed and it came. Didn't seem to have to walk just . . . came over to my . . . bed and . . . smiled at where I was.

PAUSE.

And then it said . . . [IN A WHISPER] "Emily . . . we're glad you changed your mind."

PAUSE.

And then . . . it turned and left.

AMY: Was it a doctor? [MRS. STILSON SHAKES HER HEAD] One of the staff? [MRS. STILSON SHAKES HER HEAD] How do you know?

MRS. STILSON: I just know.

PAUSE.

Then . . . I left my body.

AMY: *What?*

MRS. STILSON [WITH GREAT EXCITEMENT]: I was on the
. . . what's the name over me—

AMY: Ceiling?

MRS. STILSON: Yes! I was floating like a . . .

AMY: Cloud?

MRS. STILSON SHAKES HER HEAD.

Bird?

MRS. STILSON: Yes, up there at the—[SHE SEARCHES
FOR THE WORD; FINDS IT]—ceiling, and I looked down and
I was still there in my bed! Wasn't even scared, which you'd
think I would be . . . And I thought, wow! this is the life isn't
it?

SOUND OF WIND.

LIGHTS BEGIN TO CHANGE.

AMY RECEDES INTO THE DARKNESS.

*It comes now without my asking . . . Amy is still beside me
but I am somewhere else. I'm not scared. It has taken me,
and it's clear again. Something is about to happen.*

PAUSE.

AMY NOW COMPLETELY GONE.

MRS. STILSON IN A NARROW SPOT OF LIGHT,
DARKNESS ALL AROUND.

*I am in a plane, a Curtiss Jenny, and it's night. Winter. Snow
is falling. Feel the tremble of the wings! How I used to walk
out on them! Could I have really done—* . . . *Yes. What I'd
do, I'd strap myself with a tether to the stays, couldn't see
the tether from below, then out I'd climb! Oh my, but it was
wonderful! I could feel the wind! shut my eyes, all alone—
FEEL THE SOARING!*

THE WIND GROWS STRONGER.

THEN THE WIND DIES AWAY.

SILENCE.

SHE NOTICES THE CHANGE.

MRS. STILSON: *But this is in another time. Where I've been
also* . . . *It is night and no one else is in the plane. Is it* . . .
remembering?

PAUSE.

No . . . *No, I'm simply there again!*

PAUSE.

And I'm lost . . . *I am lost, completely lost, have to get to* . . .
*somewhere, Omaha I think. The radio is out, or rather for
some reason picks up only Bucharest. Clouds all around, no
stars only snow, don't possess a clue to where I am, flying
blind, soon be out of gas* . . . *And then the clouds open up a
bit, just a bit, and lights appear below, faint, a hint, like
torches. Down I drop! heart pounding with relief, with joy,
hoping for a landing place, I'll take anything—a field, a street,
and down I drop! No place to land* . . . *It's a town but the
smallest—one tiny street is all, three street lamps, no one on
the street, all deserted* . . . *just a street and some faint light*

*in the middle of darkness. Nothing. Still, down I go! Maybe I
can find a name on a railroad station, find out where I am!
. . . But I see nothing I can read . . . So I begin to circle,
though I know I'm wasting fuel and I'll crash if I keep this up!
But somehow, I just can't tear myself away! Though I know I
should pull back on the stick, get the nose up, head north
into darkness—Omaha must be north! But no, I keep circling
this one small silly street in this one small town . . . I'm
scared to leave it, that's what, as if I guess once away from
it I'll be inside something empty, black, and endless . . .*

PAUSE.

*So I keep circling—madness!—but I love it, what I see below!
And I just can't bring myself to give it up, it's that simple—
just can't bring myself to give it up!*

PAUSE.

*Then I know I have to. It's a luxury I can't afford. Fuel is
running low, almost gone, may be too late anyway, so—*

PAUSE.

*I pull the nose up, kick the rudder, bank, and head out into
darkness all in terror! GOD, BUT IT TAKES EFFORT! JUST
DON'T WANT TO DO IT! . . . But I do.*

PAUSE.

[SUDDENLY CALM] *Actually, odd thing, once I did, broke
free, got into the dark, found I wasn't even scared . . . Or
was I?* [SLIGHT LAUGH] *Can't remember . . . Wonder where
that town was . . . ?*

PAUSE.

Got to Omaha all right.

PAUSE.

Was it Omaha . . . ?

PAUSE.

Yes, I think so . . . Yes, Topeka, that was it!

PAUSE.

God, but it was wonderful! [SLIGHT LAUGH] *Awful scary sometimes, though!*

AMY SEEN IN THE DISTANCE.

AMY: Emily! Emily, are you all right!

SUDDEN, SHARP, TERRIFYING FLAPPING SOUND.

MRS. STILSON GASPS.

AMY DISAPPEARS.

MRS. STILSON [RAPIDLY]: *Around! There here spins saw it rumple chumps and jumps outgoes inside up and . . . takes it, gives it, okay . . .*

PAUSE.

[EASIER] *Touch her for me, would you?*

PAUSE.

[EVEN EASIER] *Oh my, yes, and here it goes then out . . . there I think on . . . wings? Yes . . .*

PAUSE.

[SOFTLY, FAINT SMILE] *Thank you.*

NO TRACE OF TERROR.

MUSIC. HINT OF BELLS.

LIGHTS TO BLACK.

SILENCE.